THE pie & tart COLLECTION

ARTISAN BAKING FOR THE
PIE AND TART ENTHUSIAST

BRIAN HART HOFFMAN

83
PRESS

THE pie & tart COLLECTION

83 Press
1900 International Park Drive, Suite 50
Birmingham, Alabama 35243
83press.com

ISBN: 978-1-940772-91-2
Printed in China

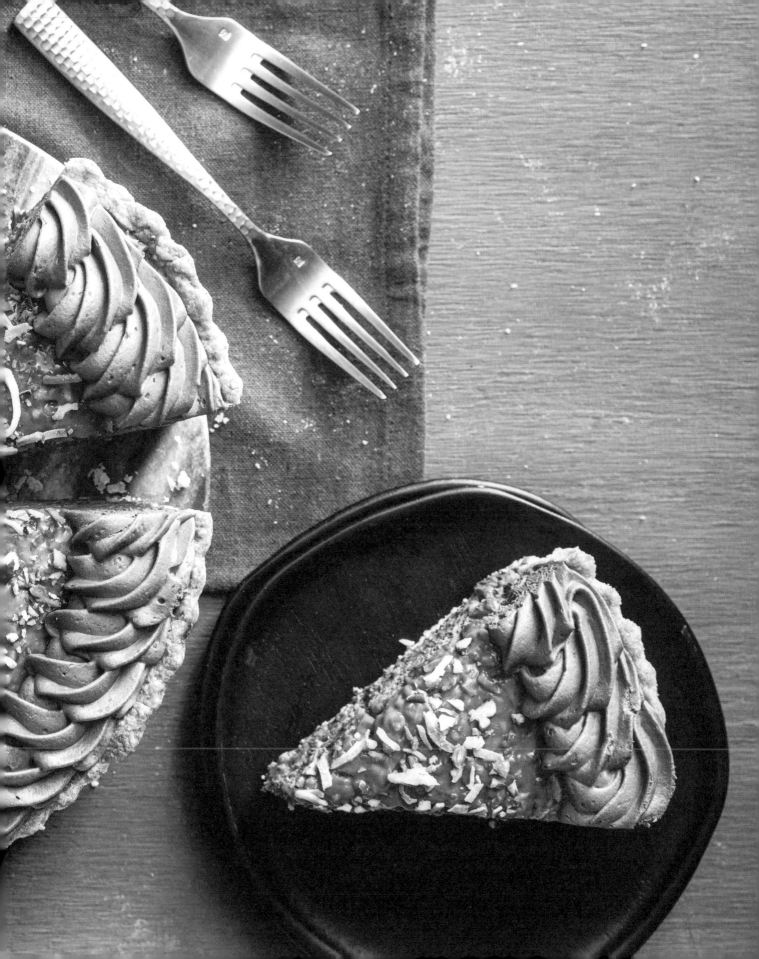

contents —————————————————————

AT LAST: THE ULTIMATE COOKBOOK FOR
PIES AND TARTS.

I've indulged in some of the finest desserts this world has to offer, but there are few more soul-warming than a slice of homemade pie. Growing up in the South, I was raised on some incredible heirloom pies. I can well remember the taste of my mother's peach pie, still warm from the oven and brimming with plump fruit and spices under a buttery lattice crust. It was one of the first baked goods that sparked my love affair with baking.

This cookbook is a loving tribute to all the wonders a freshly baked-from-scratch pie or tart can bring to the table. Each chapter covers a key piece of the pie or tart puzzle. One of my absolute favorite chapters is the "FOMO Pies." This chapter highlights the pies and tarts that evoke a baker's fear of missing out (FOMO). These are the have-to-bake-right-now recipes that keep us awake at night—right up until we scratch that sweet itch. This chapter has all the internet breaking recipes you won't be able to resist. The In-Flight Pie is an ode to my years as a flight attendant, transforming the classic snack of cookies, coffee, and peanuts into a creamy pie. A particularly stunning entry? Banana Pudding Meringue Pie that turns the iconic recipe upside down—literally. A baked meringue crust cradles a filling of pudding and bananas, and a vanilla wafer crown tops it off.

If you're looking to try your hand at something more traditional, give our "Classic Combos" chapter a spin. You can expect to find tried-and-true favorites, like our Honey Nut Pie and Strawberries and Cream Pie. Stephen's Buttermilk Pie is a particularly beloved recipe to me. It's an heirloom recipe from my husband's family. I've enjoyed it during many holiday occasions and couldn't wait to bring it to my fellow bakers. Of course, we have plenty of recipes to satisfy the wanderlust baker in you as well. "Around the World in Pies" helps shine a light on the pie traditions cherished across the globe, like the UK's banoffee pie and Hong Kong's egg tarts.

Then, we bring it home with our "Retro Revamp" chapter, where vintage pies receive a 21st-century reboot. If you've ever wondered how to improve upon apple pie, look no further than our modern marvel, Apple Crumb Pie. Made expertly creamy with crème fraîche (praise!), this pie will become the satiny standard all other pies will be compared to. Looking to take pies to the next level? "When Cake Becomes Pie" is the chapter for you. This collection reimagines iconic cakes like red velvet, Hummingbird, and even Black Forest into pies packed with dreamy fillings and divinely crisp crusts. Finally, our "Anything but the Pie Plate" chapter proves you don't need a pie plate to create the perfect crust-meets-filling experience. From galettes to hand pies, these recipes think outside of the plate.

But this cookbook collection goes beyond offering foolproof, test kitchen-approved recipes. I, of all people, know that pie-baking can be an intense task. But our goal is to help you master this art, sidestepping common pie issues and problems, guiding you every step of the way so you can create baked goods that look great and taste even better. With this fabulous reference never far from reach, beautiful pies and tarts are within your grasp.

So, without further ado, tie on your aprons and preheat your ovens. It's time to embrace the buttery, beautiful world of artisan pies and tarts.

PIES 101

BEFORE YOU GET TO THE RECIPES, TAKE A MOMENT TO REVIEW SOME OF THE CORNERSTONES OF THE PIE-MAKING TECHNIQUE, FROM THE TOOLS OF THE TRADE TO HOW TO BUILD YOUR PERFECT CRUST.

TOOLS OF THE TRADE

FEW DESSERTS CAN OUTSHINE A FRESH SLICE OF HOMEMADE PIE, AND LUCKILY, THESE SOUGHT-AFTER TREATS DO NOT REQUIRE A LOAD OF FANCY EQUIPMENT. WE'LL GO OVER THE SIMPLE TOOLS OF THE TRADE THAT WILL HAVE YOU MASTERING PIES AND TARTS.

THE WEIGH TO OUR HEARTS

If we could confess our love for one kitchen tool, it would be the digital kitchen scale. For consistency, the scale removes most variabilities caused by measuring cups and spoons, which can potentially impact recipes. For recipes like pie dough, 1 tablespoon (15 grams) water can mean the difference between a perfectly tender and flaky crust and a tough and lackluster one. Once you make the initial investment in a digital kitchen scale, it can be used for every recipe thereafter, improving your baking game with each effortlessly measured gram. No scale? Measuring cups and spoons will still work, of course, but make sure you scoop and level ingredients properly, aiming for consistency in measuring.

ON A ROLL

Before adding pie weights to the piecrust for par-baking, you will want to line the dough with aluminum foil or parchment paper. Foil is also necessary during baking to shield piecrusts that are browning too quickly. There are also specialized piecrust shields available for purchase that will protect the crust from becoming too dark.

STAYING IN SHAPE

When blind-baking (baking a piecrust before you add the filling), use ceramic pie weights to help maintain the crust's shape. Poured into your parchment paper- or foil-lined crust, these dense spheres nestle into nooks and properly weigh down your crust, whether you're using a regular or deep-dish pie plate. No pie weights? Opt for pouring in a 2-pound bag of dried uncooked beans or rice. You can also bag them up post-bake and reuse them another day.

CUTTING TO THE CHASE

Pastry blenders, also known as pastry cutters, are simply a handle supporting a loop of dull metal blades or wires. As you press the tool into the mixture, the blades effortlessly cut through butter and offer the most control. No pastry blender? Find two forks. Cutting in butter (or other fat) sans pastry blender is super simple. Use the tines of the forks to cut in fat until pieces reach the right size. If needed, the forks can then be used to stir in wet ingredients. Although you may need a bit more elbow grease, this method is still efficient and easy.

JUST ROLL WITH IT

From classic handled rolling pins to dowel-shaped pins, the rolling pin is essential in pie-making. Our go-to is most often the wooden French rolling pin, which features tapered ends that allow for easy circular rotation—perfect for rolling out piecrusts. No rolling pin? Reach for a wine bottle. When you are without a rolling pin, an empty, straight-sided wine bottle makes a great stand-in. Its cylindrical body and long, straight sides offer just the right shape and leverage. Just nix any labels and give the bottle a wash, or wrap it in plastic wrap if you're tight on time. Sans liquid works best, but full, unopened bottles will also work in a pinch.

STRAIGHT AS AN ARROW

To cut pie dough into perfect strips for a lattice design, pastry wheels and pastry crimpers (with fluted edges) are handy. Not in your wheelhouse? A pizza cutter or sharp knife and a ruler will lead you to straight strip-making success. Speaking of a ruler, it's extremely helpful for measuring and spacing out lattice strips, so keep one on hand.

CRESTLESS CRUST

When it comes to tart and cookie crusts, pastry tampers are useful gadgets to pack down the crumbs tightly. The tamps are normally made of wood and are somewhat shaped like a barbell. No tamp? Grab a straight-sided glass or measuring cup and proceed as desired.

PICK YOUR PAN

WHEN CHOOSING A PIE PLATE OR TART PAN, THE MOST IMPORTANT THING TO REMEMBER IS THAT YOUR CRUST NEEDS TO COOK FAST. ALL SHAPE AND FLAKINESS WILL BE LOST IF THE FAT MELTS BEFORE THE PROTEIN STRUCTURE STARTS TO SET.

GLASS plates conduct heat evenly, giving your crusts the most thorough bake. While other materials bake by heat conduction only, glass bakes by both conduction and radiant heat energy. This allows the heat to go directly through glass to the crust.

CERAMIC plates are the most beautiful and also conduct heat fairly evenly, but unlike glass, you can't see through them to determine if your crust is done.

METAL pans brown crusts more quickly because they become hotter in the oven. Get one with a dull finish rather than a shiny one. (Dark or dull metal pans absorb heat and bake faster than shiny pans.) Heavier metal pans made of a good heat conductor, like aluminum, give you a more evenly baked crust than thinner, less conductive metal surfaces like tin.

REGULAR AND DEEP-DISH pie plates vary only slightly in dimensions. A regular pie plate measures approximately 9 inches in diameter and 1¾ inches deep. A deep-dish plate can be between 9 and 10 inches in diameter and is greater than 1¾ inches deep. To accommodate a recipe for a regular-size pie to fit a deep-dish pie plate, increase the dough and filling by approximately 50% and increase the bake time as needed.

CUTTING THE FAT

TO CREATE TENDER, FLAKY PIECRUSTS, CUTTING COLD BUTTER INTO FLOUR UNTIL YOU HAVE PERFECT TINY LUMPS IS ESSENTIAL. CUTTING IN BUTTER GUARANTEES THAT THE COLD PIECES OF FAT MELT IN THE OVEN, CREATING STEAM, MOISTURE, AND, IDEALLY, PERFECTLY FLAKY LAYERS. WHETHER YOU PREFER TO USE YOUR HANDS, A PASTRY BLENDER, OR A FOOD PROCESSOR, WE DIVE DEEP INTO THE THREE MAIN METHODS, HIGHLIGHTING THEIR PROS AND CONS.

METHOD: PASTRY BLENDER

Begin with cold butter, cold flour, and a cold pastry blender (refrigerate, if necessary). Slice cold butter into cubes or pats with a sharp knife. Scatter butter over flour in a wide, shallow bowl. Press down on butter with pastry blender, working up and down until all butter pieces are small pea-size lumps and covered in flour.

PRO: This method allows you to properly control the exact size of the butter lumps without adding heat from your hands.

CON: Because it takes more time to manually slice in the butter, you risk having the butter come to room temperature during the process.

METHOD: BY HAND

Begin with cold butter, cold flour, and cold hands (plunged in an ice water bath and dried, if necessary). Slice cold butter into cubes or pats with a sharp knife. Scatter butter over flour in a wide, shallow bowl. Using your thumbs and fingertips, rub butter into flour in a snapping motion until all butter pieces are small pea-size lumps and covered in flour.

PRO: This method offers you the greatest amount of control in determining the size of the butter pieces, and it's the best way to make sure you're not overworking the dough.

CON: The heat from your hands will threaten softening the cold butter, not to mention this process is the most time-consuming of the three.

METHOD: FOOD PROCESSOR

Begin with cold butter and cold flour. Slice cold butter into cubes or pats with a sharp knife. Scatter butter over flour in the work bowl of a food processor. Pulse until all butter pieces are small pea-size lumps and covered in flour, 5 to 10 times.

PRO: The fastest and most efficient method of the bunch, processing your butter into the flour ensures even incorporation without bringing the heat of your hands or the room into the equation.

CON: If you're not keeping an eye on it, you can overprocess the mixture and begin to cream it. Once the mixture is overprocessed, you'll be unable to get those ideal lumps of butter back, so be prepared to give this step your undivided attention.

PAR-BAKING

PAR-BAKING IS A TECHNIQUE WHERE THE CRUST IS PARTIALLY BAKED BEFORE FILLING. THIS IS THE PREFERRED METHOD FOR FILLINGS THAT CONTAIN A LARGE PORTION OF LIQUID IN ORDER TO PREVENT A SOGGY BOTTOM. THE GOAL OF PAR-BAKING IS TO JUST SEAL THE CRUST, BAKING UNTIL THE CRUST APPEARS LIGHT-COLORED AND DRY, WITHOUT BAKING IT COMPLETELY THROUGH.

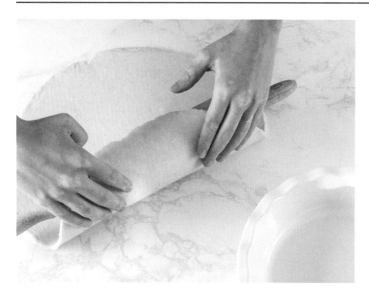

1. Roll out your pie dough to the diameter and width the recipe calls for. To transfer to your pie plate, gently roll the pie dough, like a scroll, around your rolling pin. Then gently lift and unroll the wrapped pie dough over the pie plate.

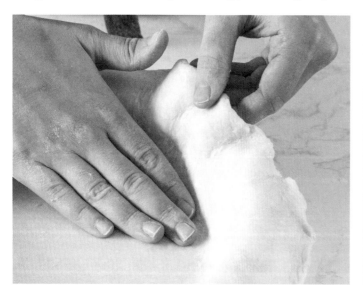
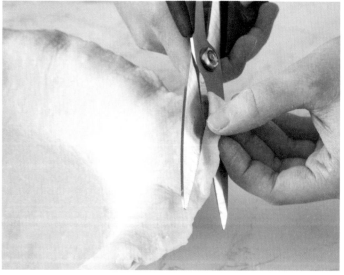

2. Press into bottom and up sides. Trim edges to ½ inch beyond edge of plate, if needed. Fold edges under, and roll down to edge of plate.

3. Crimp, if desired. To create a fluted edge, take the forefinger and thumb of one hand, and hold them about 1 inch apart touching the outside edge of the dough. Take the knuckle of your forefinger of the opposite hand and push the inside edge gently into the two fingers to create a fluted design. Continue, moving around the edge of the dough.

Alternatively, use the tines of a fork or a crimping tool to gently press into the outer edges of the dough, creating an even, rippled trim.

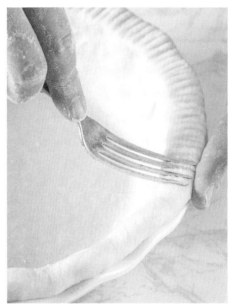

4. Lightly dock (prick) the prepared crust with a fork. Docking is simply using a fork or a wooden pick to make several small holes on the bottom of the unbaked piecrust. Without the holes, steam builds up under the crust, causing ballooning and outright unruliness. The perforations are large enough to allow steam to escape but small enough that filling will not leak through.

5. Top with a piece of foil, shiny side up, pressing excess under rim of plate. Alternatively, line with a sheet of parchment paper. Add pie weights to fill three-fourths full. Pie weights are going to be your trusty pantry tool. You can purchase reusable ceramic or metal pie weights online or at specialty stores, but dried beans and rice work equally as well and can be used repeatedly. Proceed with recipe as directed.

LATTICE PRACTICE

A CLASSIC LATTICE-TOP PIECRUST ADDS DIMENSION AND INTEREST TO YOUR PIES. COLD INGREDIENTS AND LIMITED HANDLING CREATE THE FLAKIEST CRUST, SO IT'S IMPORTANT TO BE METHODICAL WHEN GETTING YOUR DOUGH READY TO BAKE. WHEN ROLLING OUT YOUR DOUGH, USING A DOWEL OR FRENCH ROLLING PIN WITHOUT HANDLES IS BEST. BE CAREFUL NOT TO USE TOO MUCH FLOUR, OR YOUR CRUST WILL BE TOO TOUGH. FOLLOW THESE STEPS TO CREATE A BEAUTIFUL, OVEN-READY PIE.

1. Roll chilled dough from center outward using firm steady pressure. Avoid pressing down on edges so they don't become too thin. Give pie dough a 90-degree turn (quarter turn), and roll again. Lightly flour underneath dough as necessary to prevent sticking. If dough becomes too soft or warm, return it to refrigerator for 15 minutes before working again.

2. Repeat rolling and turning steps until dough is wide enough to overhang pie plate by 1 to 2 inches. For a standard 9-inch pie plate, we roll the crust into a 12-inch circle. To transfer dough to plate, place your rolling pin about 2 inches from top of rolled-out dough circle. Fold top edge of dough over rolling pin, and turn once to loosely roll around pin. Lift the pin; carefully move to middle of the plate, and unfold the dough.

3. Gently lift dough around edges, and press into corners of plate. Let the dough fall into the pan rather than stretching it into place. Let excess dough hang over edge.

4. On a lightly floured surface, roll remaining dough into a 12-inch square. Cut into 6 (2-inch-wide) strips. Place 3 dough strips vertically on pie, spacing evenly apart.

5. Fold back center vertical strip, and place a strip horizontally across first strips. Unfold vertical folded strip.

6. Fold back alternating vertical strips, and place another dough strip horizontally across vertical strips, spacing evenly. Unfold folded strips. Repeat steps 5 and 6 until lattice design is complete. If dough becomes too soft or warm, return it to refrigerator for 15 minutes before working again.

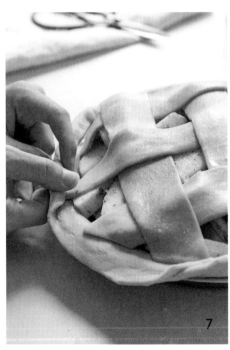

7. Using sharp kitchen scissors, trim lattice until it meets the inside of the plate's lip. Trim overhang to ½ inch beyond the plate's lip. Roll trimmed overhang over so it is even with inside lip of the plate, pressing down to make it adhere.

8. Create fluted ridges perpendicular to edge of pie plate with one hand on the inside of the edge and one hand on the outside. Using thumb of your inside hand, push the dough between the thumb and forefinger of your outside hand to form a "U" shape with the dough. Repeat this motion around the edge, spacing your flutes about 1 inch apart.

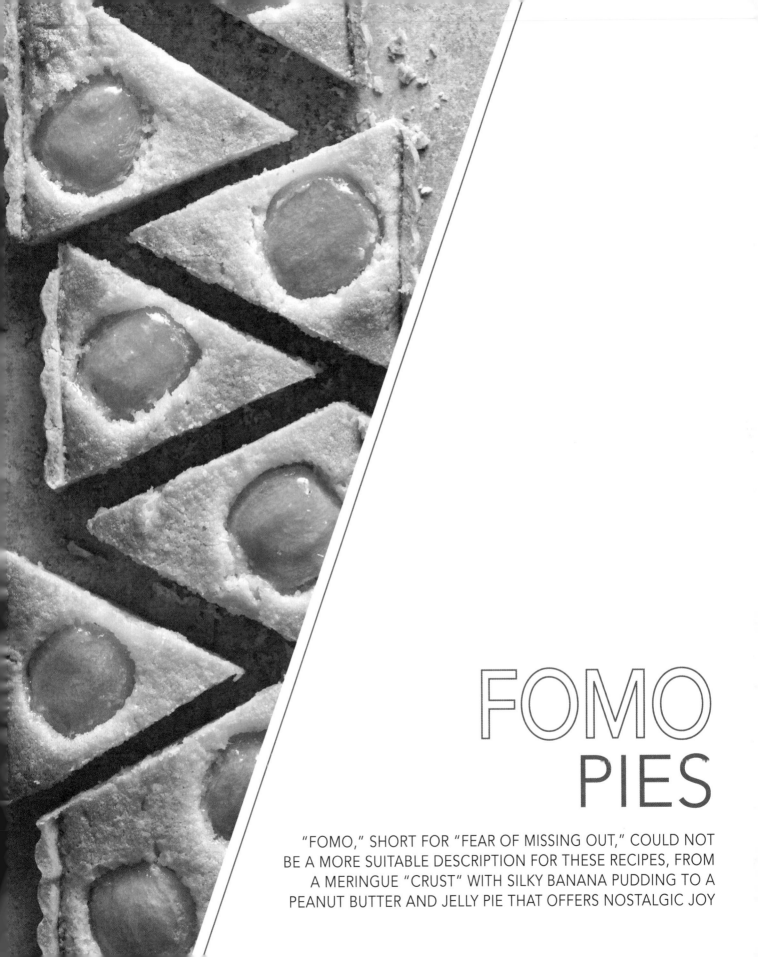

FOMO
PIES

"FOMO," SHORT FOR "FEAR OF MISSING OUT," COULD NOT
BE A MORE SUITABLE DESCRIPTION FOR THESE RECIPES, FROM
A MERINGUE "CRUST" WITH SILKY BANANA PUDDING TO A
PEANUT BUTTER AND JELLY PIE THAT OFFERS NOSTALGIC JOY

SPICED CHOCOLATE FUDGE PIE

Makes 1 (9-inch) pie

Guajillo chili and ground red pepper give this fudge pie spicy depth and a kick. Velvety cocoa notes and a light dusting of confectioners' sugar curb the heat.

Pâte Brisée (recipe on page 63)
½ cup (120 grams) heavy whipping cream
½ cup (120 grams) whole milk
¼ cup (57 grams) unsalted butter
5 ounces (150 grams) chopped semisweet chocolate
3 ounces (86 grams) Mexican chili chocolate*, chopped
1½ cups (300 grams) granulated sugar
¾ cup (64 grams) unsweetened cocoa powder
¼ cup (31 grams) all-purpose flour
2 tablespoons (18 grams) cornmeal
½ teaspoon (1.5 grams) kosher salt
¼ teaspoon ground red pepper
2 large eggs (100 grams)
3 large egg yolks (56 grams)
1 tablespoon (15 grams) apple cider vinegar
Garnish: confectioners' sugar

1. On a lightly floured surface, roll Pâte Brisée into a 12-inch circle. Transfer to a 9-inch pie plate, pressing into bottom and up sides. Trim excess dough to ½ inch beyond edge of plate. Fold edges under. Using kitchen scissors, make a ¼-inch-thick (45-degree) cut into folded edge, being careful not to cut all the way through the dough. Lay dough piece over to one side. Make another ¼-inch-thick cut, and lay to the other side. Repeat procedure around pie until you reach the first cut. Freeze for 20 minutes.
2. Preheat oven to 350°F (180°C).

3. In a medium saucepan, cook cream, milk, butter, and chocolates over medium-low heat, stirring frequently, until chocolate is melted and smooth. Remove from heat. Let stand for 2 minutes.
4. In a medium bowl, whisk together granulated sugar, cocoa, flour, cornmeal, salt, and red pepper. Add sugar mixture to chocolate mixture, and whisk to combine. Add eggs, egg yolks, and vinegar, whisking until well combined. Spoon filling into prepared crust.
5. Bake until center is set, 35 to 45 minutes, covering crust with foil after 20 minutes of baking to prevent excess browning. Let cool on a wire rack for 20 minutes; serve warm. Garnish with confectioners' sugar, if desired.

We used Taza Guajillo Chili Mexican Chocolate.

APRICOT FRANGIPANE TART

Makes 1 (14x4-inch) tart

We love the extra-crunchy texture almond flour lends to this not-too-sweet dessert's crust. Smooth frangipane, an almond pastry cream, adds another nutty element, and is a great base for the fresh, juicy apricots in both taste and texture.

1	cup (125 grams) all-purpose flour
1¼	cups (120 grams) almond flour, divided
½	cup (100 grams) plus 1 teaspoon (4 grams) granulated sugar, divided
½	teaspoon (1.5 grams) kosher salt
7	tablespoons (98 grams) cold unsalted butter
3	tablespoons (45 grams) cold water
½	cup (113 grams) unsalted butter, softened
2	large eggs (100 grams)
1	teaspoon (5 grams) dark rum
¼	teaspoon (1 gram) almond extract
4	small apricots (250 grams), peeled and halved
3	tablespoons (60 grams) apricot jam, warmed and strained

1. In the work bowl of a food processor, place all-purpose flour, ¼ cup (24 grams) almond flour, 1 teaspoon (4 grams) sugar, and salt; process until combined. Add cold butter, and pulse until mixture is crumbly. With processor running, add 2 tablespoons (30 grams) cold water in a slow, steady stream just until dough comes together but is not sticky; add up to remaining 1 tablespoon (15 grams) cold water, 1 teaspoon (5 grams) at a time, if needed. Shape dough into a disk, and wrap in plastic wrap. Refrigerate for at least 30 minutes.

2. In the bowl of a stand mixer fitted with the paddle attachment, beat butter and remaining ½ cup (100 grams) sugar at medium speed until creamy, 3 to 4 minutes, stopping to scrape sides of bowl. Reduce mixer speed to low. Add eggs, one at a time, beating just until combined after each addition. Stir in rum and almond extract. Stir in remaining 1 cup (96 grams) almond flour just until combined.

3. Preheat oven to 350°F (180°C). Butter and flour a 14x4-inch tart pan.

4. On a lightly floured surface, roll dough into a 15x5-inch rectangle. Transfer to prepared pan, pressing into bottom and up sides. Trim excess dough. Freeze for 10 minutes.

5. Top dough with a piece of parchment paper, letting ends extend over edges of pan. Add pie weights.

6. Bake just until edges are set, 10 to 12 minutes. Carefully remove parchment and weights, and bake 2 minutes more. Let cool. Spread filling into prepared crust. Top with apricots, cut side down.

7. Place tart pan on a rimmed baking sheet to catch any drips. Bake until lightly browned, 40 to 45 minutes. Let cool for 20 minutes before removing from pan. Brush tops of apricots with jam before serving.

CHAI SPICE CARAMEL PIE

Makes 1 (9-inch) pie

This luxurious pie offers a medley of spicy, salty, sharp, and sweet. Our crisp Gingersnap Crumb Crust is the perfect cradle for the light, velvety caramel filling topped with billowy, torched meringue.

2   cups (480 grams) whole milk
1   cinnamon stick
1   (3x1-inch) strip orange peel
1   vanilla bean, split lengthwise, seeds scraped and reserved
½   teaspoon (1.5 gram) black peppercorns
¼   teaspoon whole cloves
¼   teaspoon green cardamom pods
1   whole star anise (2 grams)
1   cup (220 grams) firmly packed light brown sugar
½   cup (63 grams) all-purpose flour
4   large egg yolks (74 grams)
½   teaspoon (1.5 grams) kosher salt
1   cup (200 grams) granulated sugar
Gingersnap Crumb Crust (recipe below)
Salty Honey Meringue (recipe follows)
Garnish: flaked sea salt

1. In a medium saucepan, bring milk, cinnamon stick, orange peel, vanilla bean and reserved seeds, peppercorns, cloves, cardamom, and star anise to a boil over medium heat. Cover, remove from heat, and let steep for 20 minutes. Strain milk, discarding solids; return milk to saucepan. Whisk in brown sugar, flour, egg yolks, and kosher salt. Cook, whisking constantly, until thickened. Remove from heat to keep custard from overcooking. You want custard as hot as possible, so do not give it time to cool down before adding caramel in next step.
2. In a small nonstick skillet, cook granulated sugar over medium heat, stirring occasionally, until deep amber colored. Whisking milk mixture constantly, slowly add caramel. Strain through a fine-mesh sieve into prepared Gingersnap Crumb Crust. Smooth top, and let cool for 10 minutes. Cover with a piece of plastic wrap, pressing wrap directly onto surface of filling to prevent a skin form forming, and refrigerate until set, at least 3 hours or up to 2 days. Top with Salty Honey Meringue, and toast with a kitchen torch. Garnish with sea salt, if desired.

GINGERSNAP CRUMB CRUST
Makes 1 (9-inch) crust

Substitute any of your favorite crisp cookies for the gingersnaps. The recipe method will stay the same, but you may have to adjust the amount of butter and sugar if the cookie has a different sugar or fat content than gingersnaps. Add the sugar to taste, and add the butter gradually, mixing only until crumbs are slightly moist.

2   cups (200 grams) gingersnap crumbs
¼   cup (55 grams) firmly packed light brown sugar
½   teaspoon (1.5 grams) kosher salt
¼   cup (57 grams) unsalted butter, melted

1. Preheat oven to 350°F (180°C).
2. In a medium bowl, whisk together gingersnap crumbs, brown sugar, and salt. Add melted butter, stirring until well combined. Using the bottom of a measuring cup, gently press crumb mixture into bottom and up sides of a 9-inch pie plate.
3. Bake for 10 minutes. Let cool completely on a wire rack.

Note: *For the best results, the crumbs you use should be fine, like the texture of a nut meal. You should not see any chunks.*

SALTY HONEY MERINGUE
Makes about 4 cups

4   large egg whites (120 grams)
⅓   cup (73 grams) firmly packed light brown sugar
⅓   cup (113 grams) clover honey
½   teaspoon (1.5 grams) kosher salt

1. In the top of a double boiler, whisk together all ingredients. Cook over simmering water, whisking constantly, until sugar is dissolved and a candy thermometer registers 140°F (60°C), 5 to 7 minutes. Transfer to the bowl of a stand mixer fitted with the whisk attachment, and beat at high speed until stiff peaks form, about 10 minutes. Use immediately.

CARAMELIZED WHITE CHOCOLATE CHESS PIE

Makes 1 (9-inch) pie

Recipe by Jesse Szewczyk

Chess pie is delicious, but it's not always the prettiest—so dust the top of this baby in confectioners' sugar, and call it a day. Chess pie will form a crunchy top while it bakes. This is a sign of a good chess pie and to be expected, but it can also make the surface crack and sink. If you want your pie to have a flatter top, bake it in a water bath, and let cool in the warm oven before removing it.

Pie Dough (recipe follows)
½   cup (113 grams) unsalted butter, cubed
4   ounces (113 grams) Caramelized White Chocolate (recipe follows), coarsely chopped
1   cup (200 grams) granulated sugar
4   large eggs (200 grams)
2   tablespoons (18 grams) yellow cornmeal
1   teaspoon (4 grams) vanilla extract
¼   teaspoon kosher salt
1   tablespoon (7 grams) confectioners' sugar

1. Preheat oven to 350°F (180°C).
2. On a lightly floured surface, roll Pie Dough into a 12-inch circle. Transfer to a 9-inch pie pan, pressing into bottom and up sides. Trim excess dough to ½ inch beyond edge of pan. Fold edges under, and crimp as desired. Prick bottom of dough all over with a fork. Freeze for 15 minutes.
3. Top dough with a piece of parchment paper, letting ends extend over edges of pan. Add pie weights.
4. Bake for 15 minutes; carefully remove parchment and weights. Let cool completely on a wire rack. Reduce oven temperature to 325°F (170°C).
5. In the top of a double boiler, combine butter and Caramelized White Chocolate. Cook over simmering water, stirring frequently, until melted, about 5 minutes. Remove from heat; add granulated sugar, eggs, cornmeal, vanilla, and salt, whisking until smooth. Pour filling into prepared crust.
6. Bake until center is set and no longer jiggly, about 40 minutes. Let cool for 2 hours. To make a stripe pattern, lay 1-inch strips of parchment paper over pie. Dust with confectioners' sugar, and carefully remove parchment. Serve immediately, or refrigerate until ready to serve. Let stand at room temperature for 1 hour before serving.

PIE DOUGH
Makes 1 (9-inch) crust

1½   cups (188 grams) all-purpose flour
1   teaspoon (4 grams) granulated sugar
½   teaspoon (1.5 grams) kosher salt
½   cup (113 grams) unsalted butter, cubed
4 to 5 tablespoons (60 to 75 grams) cold water

1. In the work bowl of a food processor, place flour, sugar, and salt; pulse until combined. Add butter, and pulse until mixture is crumbly. With processor running, add 4 to 5 tablespoons (60 to 75 grams) cold water, 1 tablespoon (15 grams) at a time, just until a dry dough forms.
2. Turn out dough, and shape into a disk. Wrap in plastic wrap, and refrigerate for 1 hour.

CARAMELIZED WHITE CHOCOLATE
Makes about 2 cups

16   ounces (454 grams) white chocolate baking chips
¼   teaspoon kosher salt

1. Preheat oven to 250°F (130°C).
2. In a completely dry 9-inch round cake pan, combine white chocolate and salt.
3. Bake until smooth and deep golden and smells like toasted marshmallows, 30 minutes to 1 hour, stirring every 10 minutes. (At times, it will look very dry and chalky, but keep stirring until smooth.) Pour onto a parchment paper-lined rimmed baking sheet, and let set for at least 7 hours or up to overnight.
4. Break into pieces, and store in an airtight container for up to 1 months.

Photo by Mark Weinberg

BANANA PUDDING MERINGUE PIE

Makes 1 (9-inch) pie

A classic turned upside down, our delicious take on this fruit-studded cream pie inspired by Erin Jeanne McDowell's #mydreampie challenge is totally bananas. Vanilla wafers are crumbled into a fluffy meringue, which is piped into a pie plate and then baked. The vanilla-scented meringue shell turns both crunchy and chewy—a flawless vessel for holding creamy homemade vanilla pudding and fresh-cut banana slices. A special shoutout to Rose Levy Beranbaum for this incredible meringue shell technique.

2   cups (480 grams) whole milk
½   cup (100 grams) granulated sugar
¼   cup (32 grams) cornstarch
¾   teaspoon (2.25 grams) kosher salt
3   large egg yolks (56 grams)
1   large egg (50 grams)
2   tablespoons (28 grams) unsalted butter, cubed and softened
½   teaspoon (3 grams) vanilla bean paste
3   large firm ripe bananas (566 grams), sliced crosswise ¼ inch thick
¾   teaspoon (3.75 grams) fresh lemon juice
Vanilla Wafer-Meringue Crust (recipe follows)
1⅓ cups (120 grams) roughly crushed vanilla wafers (32 to 34 wafers), divided
1   cup (240 grams) cold heavy whipping cream
¼   cup (30 grams) confectioners' sugar
Garnish: banana slices, vanilla wafers

1. In a medium saucepan, heat milk over medium heat until steaming. (Do not boil.)
2. In a medium bowl, whisk together granulated sugar, cornstarch, and salt. Whisk in egg yolks and egg until well combined. Gradually whisk half of warm milk into sugar mixture. Pour sugar mixture into remaining warm milk in pan, and bring to a boil over medium heat, whisking constantly. Cook, whisking constantly, until thickened, mixture no longer tastes starchy, and an instant-read thermometer registers 185°F (85°C), about 3 minutes. Remove from heat.
3. Add butter to milk mixture in two additions, stirring until combined; stir in vanilla bean paste. Pour and press mixture through a fine-mesh sieve into a large bowl, smoothing into an even layer. Cover with a piece of plastic wrap, pressing wrap directly onto surface of custard to prevent a skin from forming. Refrigerate until chilled, 3 to 4 hours or up to overnight.

4. Stir chilled filling until smooth. In a large bowl, gently stir together banana slices and lemon juice. Using a small offset spatula, spread one-third of filling (about 208 grams) in bottom of Vanilla Wafer-Meringue Crust; sprinkle half of crushed wafers evenly on top, and cover with a single layer of banana slices. Repeat layers once, piling as high as needed; cover with remaining filling, smoothing into an even layer. (Reserve any extra banana slices for garnish.) Cover and refrigerate for 20 minutes.
5. In the bowl of a stand mixer fitted with the whisk attachment, beat cold cream and confectioners' sugar at medium speed until medium-stiff peaks form. Spoon and spread whipped cream mixture on top of pie, leaving a ½- to ¾-inch border around edges. Garnish with bananas and whole wafers, if desired. Serve immediately.

Vanilla Wafer-Meringue Crust

Makes 1 (9-inch) crust

½   cup (64 grams) plus 2½ teaspoons (7.5 grams) cornstarch, divided
1¼ cups (250 grams) granulated sugar
5   large egg whites (150 grams), room temperature
1   teaspoon (5 grams) fresh lemon juice
¼   teaspoon kosher salt
¾   teaspoon (4.5 grams) vanilla bean paste
⅓   cup (32 grams) very finely crushed vanilla wafers* (about 10 wafers)

1. Preheat oven to 225°F (107°C). Lightly spray a 9-inch pie plate with cooking spray. Place on a piece of parchment paper.
2. Using a small fine-mesh sieve, dust prepared pan with ½ cup (64 grams) cornstarch until completely and generously coated.. Tip and hold pan, as needed, to help coat sides. (It's OK if cornstarch is piled in spots; no need to shake out excess.)
3. In the heatproof bowl of a stand mixer, whisk together sugar, egg whites, lemon juice, salt, and remaining 2½ teaspoons (7.5 grams) cornstarch by hand. Place bowl over a saucepan of simmering water. Cook, stirring frequently and scraping sides of bowl, until sugar completely dissolves and an instant-read thermometer registers 120°F (49°C) to 130°F (54°C).
4. Carefully return bowl to stand mixer. Using the whisk attachment, beat at high speed until stiff peaks form and bowl is cool to the touch, 10 to 12 minutes, adding vanilla bean paste during last minute of mixing. Fold in crushed wafers in two additions just until combined.
5. Spoon about two-thirds of meringue mixture (about 300 grams) into a pastry bag fitted with a ½-inch round piping tip (Wilton No. 2A). Starting in center, pipe meringue in a tight, even spiral in bottom of prepared pan; starting from bottom edge and working upward, pipe meringue in rings around sides of pan.
6. Spoon remaining meringue into a pastry bag fitted with a medium open star tip (Wilton 1M). Pipe meringue decoratively around top edge of pan as desired. (Make sure your piping is supported underneath by meringue and/or edge of your pan so meringue does

not sag while baking.) Use any remaining meringue to patch holes or thin areas, smoothing with a small offset spatula, if necessary.

7. Bake until dry and firm to the touch, 1½ hours to 1 hour and 45 minutes. Turn oven off, and let meringue stand in oven with door closed for 1 hour. Let cool completely in pan on a wire rack. (It's OK if meringue surface cracks or falls slightly.) Best used same day.

To very finely crush, place vanilla wafers in a small resealable plastic bag. Using a rolling pin, crush until wafers are ground into very fine crumbs.

PRO TIP

If desired, once your meringue crust is baked and cooled, use a pastry brush to sweep away any excess cornstarch, and use a paper towel to carefully clean exposed edges of pan.

SPARKLING WINE CHOCOLATE GANACHE TART

Makes 1 (9½-inch) tart

Sparkling wine and chocolate are a winning combination, creating a tart ideal for any celebration. With a graham cracker crumb base, a semisweet ganache filling, and a sparkling wine-spiked white chocolate cream topping, this tart is chilled perfection.

1½   cups (176 grams) chocolate graham cracker crumbs (about 12 sheets)
2   tablespoons (24 grams) granulated sugar
6   tablespoons (84 grams) unsalted butter, melted
10   ounces (284 grams) 64% cacao semisweet chocolate*, finely chopped (about 1⅔ cups)
2   cups (480 grams) cold heavy whipping cream, divided
¼   teaspoon kosher salt
⅓   cup (80 grams) plus 2 tablespoons (30 grams) brut sparkling white wine, divided
6   ounces (170 grams) white chocolate*, finely chopped (about 1 cup)
Garnish: dark chocolate crunchy pearls, semisweet chocolate shavings

1. Preheat oven to 350°F (180°C). Spray a 9½-inch fluted round removable-bottom tart pan with baking spray with flour.
2. In the work bowl of a food processor, combine graham cracker crumbs and sugar; pulse until well combined. Add melted butter; pulse until well combined and mixture holds together when pinched. Press graham cracker mixture into bottom and up sides of prepared pan.
3. Bake until crust is set and fragrant, 8 to 10 minutes. Let cool completely on a wire rack.
4. In the top of a double boiler, combine semisweet chocolate, 1 cup (240 grams) cold cream, and salt. Cook over simmering water, stirring frequently, until chocolate is melted and mixture is smooth. Remove from heat; gradually whisk in ⅓ cup (80 grams) wine until smooth and well combined. Pour mixture into prepared crust. Refrigerate until filling is set, at least 3 hours or up to overnight.

5. In the clean top of a double boiler, combine white chocolate and ⅓ cup (80 grams) cold cream. Cook over simmering water, stirring frequently, until chocolate is melted and mixture is smooth. Transfer white chocolate mixture to the bowl of a stand mixer, and let cool to room temperature (70°F/21°C).
6. Using the whisk attachment, beat cooled white chocolate mixture at medium speed; gradually add remaining 2 tablespoons (30 grams) wine, beating until combined. Reduce mixer speed to medium-low; slowly add ⅓ cup (80 grams) cold cream, beating until smooth and stopping frequently to scrape sides of bowl. Increase mixer speed to medium; gradually add remaining ⅓ cup (80 grams) cold cream, beating until medium-stiff peaks form. (Whisk by hand toward end if needed; do not overmix.) Spread and swirl topping on tart as desired, being careful not to overhandle topping. Garnish with chocolate pearls and chocolate shavings, if desired. Refrigerate until topping is set, about 30 minutes. Remove from pan, and serve immediately.

We used Guittard 64% Cacao Semisweet Chocolate Baking Bars and Ghirardelli White Chocolate Baking Bars.

PEANUT BUTTER AND JELLY PIE

Makes 1 (9-inch) pie

A pie version of my favorite sandwich! This recipe is reminiscent of one I ate in Texas during a tour of their peanut-growing region. With a slightly salty crust, creamy and light peanut butter filling, and an incredible jammy topping, this pie hits all the right notes.

8	ounces (226 grams) cream cheese, softened
1	cup (256 grams) creamy peanut butter
¼	cup (50 grams) granulated sugar
¼	cup (85 grams) honey
1	cup (240 grams) cold heavy whipping cream

Cracker Crust (recipe follows)
Strawberry Jelly (recipe follows)

1. In the bowl of a stand mixer fitted with the paddle attachment, beat cream cheese and peanut butter at medium-high speed until smooth, about 3 minutes. Add sugar and honey, beating until smooth, about 2 minutes. Transfer to a large bowl.
2. Clean bowl of stand mixer. Using the whisk attachment, beat cream at medium-high speed until stiff peaks form. Fold one-third of whipped cream into cream cheese mixture until well combined. Fold in remaining whipped cream until no streaks remain. Gently scoop filling into Cracker Crust, smoothing top with a small offset spatula. Freeze until filling is firm, about 1 hour.
3. Pour and spread Strawberry Jelly in an even layer on top of pie. Freeze until jelly is set, about 1 hour.

Cracker Crust

Makes 1 (9-inch) crust

2	cups (155 grams) crushed buttery round crackers
7	tablespoons (98 grams) unsalted butter, melted
⅓	cup (73 grams) firmly packed dark brown sugar
½	teaspoon (1.5 grams) kosher salt

1. Preheat oven to 275°F (135°C)
2. In a large bowl, stir together crushed crackers, melted butter, brown sugar, and salt. Press mixture into bottom and up sides of a 9-inch pie plate. Place plate on a rimmed baking sheet.
3. Bake until set and fragrant, 20 to 25 minutes. Let cool completely on a wire rack.

Strawberry Jelly

Makes 1 cup

1	cup (370 grams) strawberry preserves
1	tablespoon (9 grams) tapioca flour
1	tablespoon (15 grams) water

1. In a medium saucepan, heat preserves until bubbles form around edges of pan, 8 to 10 minutes. (Do not boil.)
2. In a small bowl, whisk together tapioca flour and 1 tablespoon (15 grams) water to create a slurry. Add tapioca mixture to preserves, and cook until entire preserves mixture is bubbling.
3. Strain mixture through a fine-mesh sieve into a medium bowl, discarding solids. Let cool to room temperature. Use immediately.

FRUITY CEREAL TART

Makes 1 (10x2-inch) tart

Cereal lovers, this one is for you! The nostalgic flavor of your favorite fruity cereal is packed into a deep-dish tart of epic proportions.

5   cups (1,200 grams) whole milk, plus more if necessary
3   cups (150 grams) fruity crisp rice cereal*, divided
Fruity Cereal Crust (recipe follows)
1¼ cups (250 grams) granulated sugar, divided
½   cup (64 grams) cornstarch
1⅛ teaspoons (3 grams) kosher salt, divided
½   teaspoon (1 gram) ground cardamom
7   large egg yolks (130 grams)
1   large egg (50 grams)
¼   cup (57 grams) unsalted butter, cubed and softened
1   teaspoon (6 grams) vanilla bean paste, divided
Rose gel food coloring*
3   ounces (86 grams) cream cheese, softened
1   cup (240 grams) cold heavy whipping cream
Garnish: roughly crushed fruity crisp rice cereal*

1. In a large bowl, stir together milk and 2 cups (100 grams) cereal; let stand at room temperature for 1 hour, stirring occasionally. Using a fine-mesh sieve, strain cereal milk into a large, 4- or 8-cup glass liquid-measuring cup; discard solids. Add additional milk, if necessary, to yield 4 cups (960 grams) cereal milk. Set aside.
2. Let Fruity Cereal Crust stand at room temperature until slightly softened, 10 to 15 minutes (See Note).
3. Spray a tall-sided 10-inch fluted round removable-bottom tart pan with baking spray with flour.
4. On a lightly floured surface, roll Fruity Cereal Crust into a 14-inch circle (about ⅛ to ¼ inch thick), flouring rolling pin and work surface as needed. Press dough into bottom and up sides of prepared pan. (It's OK if dough tears in spots; press back together using a fingertip dipped in water to thoroughly seal any seams.) Using a small, sharp knife, trim dough flush with sides of pan; pinch sides lightly so dough sits about ⅛ to 1/16 inch above top edge of pan, and use any excess dough to patch thinner spots in crust. Cover and freeze until firm, 20 to 25 minutes
5. Preheat oven to 350°F (180°C).

6. Place prepared crust on a rimmed baking sheet. Top with parchment paper, letting ends extend over edges of pan. Add pie weights.
7. Bake until edges are lightly golden and set, 18 to 22 minutes, rotating pan halfway through baking. Carefully remove parchment and weights; using the tines of a fork, dock bottom of prepared crust. Bake until golden, dry, and set, 15 to 20 minutes more, lightly covering edges with foil to prevent excess browning, if necessary. (It's OK if crust shrinks slightly; if bottom puffs, gently push down with a spoon.) Let cool completely in pan on a wire rack.
8. In a medium saucepan, heat cereal milk over medium heat until steaming. (Do not boil.)
9. In a large bowl, whisk together 1 cup (200 grams) sugar, cornstarch, 1 teaspoon (3 grams) salt, and cardamom. Whisk in egg yolks and egg until well combined. Gradually whisk half of warm milk mixture into sugar mixture. Pour into remaining warm milk mixture in pan. Bring to a boil over medium heat, whisking constantly. Cook, whisking constantly, until thickened, mixture no longer tastes starchy, and an instant-read thermometer registers 185F (85C), about 3 minutes. Remove from heat. Stir in butter in two additions; stir in ½ teaspoon (3 grams) vanilla bean paste. Stir in food coloring until desired shade is reached. Pour and press mixture through a fine-mesh sieve into a large baking dish or bowl; smooth into an even layer. Cover with a piece of plastic wrap, pressing wrap directly onto surface of custard to prevent a skin from forming. Refrigerate for 30 minutes.
10. Roughly crush remaining 1 cup (50 grams) cereal; fold into custard. Spoon custard into prepared crust, smoothing into an even layer. Cover with a piece of plastic wrap, and refrigerate until set, 4 hours or up to overnight.
11. In the bowl of a stand mixer fitted with the whisk attachment, beat cream cheese and remaining ¼ cup (50 grams) sugar at medium speed until smooth and well combined, about 1 minute, stopping to scrape sides of bowl. Reduce mixer speed to medium-low; gradually add one-third of cold cream, remaining ½ teaspoon (3 grams) vanilla bean paste, and remaining ⅛ teaspoon salt until smooth, stopping to scrape sides of bowl. Gradually add remaining cold cream; increase mixer speed to medium, and beat until thickened and stiff peaks form. (Whisk by hand toward end, if necessary; do not overmix.)
12. Uncover tart. Using a kitchen torch, gently warm sides of pan to loosen. Remove from pan, and place on a serving plate. (Alternatively, let tart stand at room temperature for 30 minutes; remove from pan, and place on a serving plate.)
13. Spoon cream cheese mixture into a pastry bag fitted with a ½-inch round piping tip (Wilton No. 1A); pipe on top of tart as desired. Refrigerate for 20 minutes before serving. Garnish with crushed cereal, if desired.

*We used Fruity Pebbles Cereal and Wilton Rose Icing Color.

Note: *Dough refrigerated overnight may need to stand at room temperature until slightly softened, 30 to 45 minutes, before rolling.*

FRUITY CEREAL CRUST

Makes 1 (10-inch) crust

1   cup (227 grams) cold unsalted butter
2⅔ cups (333 grams) all-purpose flour
⅓   cup (16 grams) fruity crisp rice cereal*, very finely ground (see Note)
3   tablespoons (36 grams) granulated sugar
1¼ teaspoons (3.75 grams) kosher salt
½   teaspoon (1 gram) ground cardamom
3   tablespoons (45 grams) whole milk
2   large egg yolks (37 grams)
¼   teaspoon (1.5 grams) vanilla bean paste

1. Cut cold butter into ½- to ¾-inch cubes. Freeze until firm, about 10 minutes.

2. In the bowl of a stand mixer, whisk together flour, cereal, sugar, salt, and cardamom by hand. Add frozen butter; using the paddle attachment, beat at low speed until butter is broken into small pieces, 2 to 3 minutes. (If any large pieces of butter remain, squeeze between fingers to break up.)

3. In a 1-cup liquid-measuring cup, whisk together milk, egg yolks, and vanilla bean paste. With mixer on very low speed, add milk mixture to flour mixture in a slow, steady stream, beating just until moist clumps form. Transfer mixture to a large piece of plastic wrap. Using your hands, bring mixture together to form a cohesive dough. Shape dough into a 7-inch disk, and wrap in plastic wrap. Refrigerate for at least 1 hour or up to overnight.

Note: *To finely grind, place cereal in a small resealable plastic bag. Crush with a rolling pin until very finely ground.*

CHOCOLATE CHIP COOKIE PIE

Makes 1 (9-inch) pie

Is there anything more heartwarming than milk and cookies? This pie trades in classic pie dough for Chocolate Chip Cookie Dough and is finished with a creamy vanilla-scented milk-based filling.

Chocolate Chip Cookie Dough (recipe follows)
2½ cups (600 grams) whole milk
1¼ cups (250 grams) granulated sugar
5   tablespoons (40 grams) cornstarch
10   tablespoons (140 grams) unsalted butter, cubed
1¼ teaspoons (7.5 grams) vanilla bean paste
¼   teaspoon kosher salt

1. Preheat oven to 400°F (200°C).
2. Top Chocolate Chip Cookie Dough in pie plate with a piece of parchment paper, letting ends extend over edges of plate. Add pie weights.
3. Bake dough in plate until edges look dry, about 7 minutes. Carefully remove parchment and weights. Bake until crust is completely dry and set, 5 to 7 minutes more. Bake dough on baking sheet for 12 to 14 minutes. Let crust cool completely in plate on a wire rack; let baked cookie dough cool completely on pan on a wire rack. Reduce oven temperature to 375°F (190°C)
4. In a large saucepan, heat milk over medium heat until steaming, about 4 minutes. (Do not boil.)
5. In a medium bowl, whisk together sugar and cornstarch. Gently pour sugar mixture into warm milk, whisking until combined. Bring to a boil over medium heat, whisking constantly, until thickened and mixture no longer tastes starchy, about 3 minutes. Remove from heat. Whisk in butter, vanilla bean paste, and salt. Pour into prepared crust.
6. Bake until edges are set and an instant-read thermometer inserted in center registers 170°F (77°C) to 175°F (79°C), 20 to 25 minutes. Let cool completely on a wire rack, about 30 minutes. Refrigerate until fully set, about 4 hours.
7. Finely chop baked cookie dough, and sprinkle on top of pie as desired. Serve cold.

CHOCOLATE CHIP COOKIE DOUGH

Makes 2 cups

½   cup (113 grams) unsalted butter, softened
¼   cup (55 grams) firmly packed dark brown sugar
1   large egg yolk (19 grams), room temperature
1   teaspoon (4 grams) vanilla extract
1¾ cups (219 grams) all-purpose flour
1   teaspoon (3 grams) kosher salt
1   tablespoon plus 1 teaspoon (20 grams) ice water
¼   cup (43 grams) finely chopped 70% cacao dark chocolate

1. In the bowl of a stand mixer fitted with the paddle attachment, beat butter and brown sugar at medium-low speed until creamy, about 3 minutes, stopping to scrape sides of bowl. Add egg yolk and vanilla, and beat at medium speed until smooth, about 2 minutes. Add flour and salt, and beat at low speed just until combined. Add 1 tablespoon plus 1 teaspoon (20 grams) ice water, and beat just until combined and dough holds together when pressed. Add chocolate, and beat until combined.
2. On a small baking sheet lined with parchment paper, press ½ cup (115 grams) dough into a ¼-inch-thick rectangle. Refrigerate until firm, about 20 minutes.
3. Press remaining dough into bottom and up sides of a 9-inch pie plate. Refrigerate until firm, about 30 minutes.

ROASTED STRAWBERRY MILK PIE

Makes 1 (9-inch) pie

It's no secret that I've been obsessed with roasting strawberries for a number of recipes. After roasting, they get puréed and stirred into the most luscious, creamy filling. The result is the strawberry milk pie of your dreams.

- 1½ pounds (676 grams) fresh strawberries (halved or quartered, if large)
- ¾ cup (150 grams) granulated sugar, divided
- ⅛ teaspoon kosher salt
- 1½ cups (360 grams) heavy whipping cream
- 1 cup (240 grams) whole milk
- ⅓ cup (80 grams) cold water
- 2 teaspoons (8 grams) unflavored gelatin
- ½ teaspoon (2 grams) vanilla extract
- ¼ teaspoon (1 gram) almond extract
- All-Butter Piecrust (recipe follows)
- Sweetened whipped cream, to serve

1. Preheat oven to 375°F (190°C).

2. In a 13x9-inch baking dish, stir together strawberries, ¼ cup (50 grams) sugar, and salt until well combined.

3. Bake until berries are very soft (they should provide no resistance when poked with a fork) and fragrant and have released ample juices, 20 to 25 minutes, stirring after 10 minutes of baking. Let cool slightly.

4. Transfer two-thirds of roasted strawberries to the container of a blender or the work bowl of a food processor; process until smooth. Reserve and refrigerate remaining one-third of roasted strawberries and juices.

5. In a large saucepan, whisk together cream, milk, and remain ½ cup (100 grams) sugar. Stir in strawberry purée. Cook over medium-low heat, whisking frequently, just until steaming. (Do not boil.) Remove from heat.

6. In a small bowl, place ⅓ cup (80 grams) cold water; sprinkle gelatin on top. Let stand for 5 minutes. Whisk gelatin mixture into strawberry mixture until fully dissolved. Whisk in extracts. Pour mixture into All-Butter Piecrust. Refrigerate for at least 6 hours or up to overnight. Serve with whipped cream and reserved roasted strawberries and juices.

ALL-BUTTER PIECRUST

Makes 1 (9-inch) crust

- 1¼ cups (156 grams) all-purpose flour
- 1 tablespoon (12 grams) granulated sugar
- ¼ teaspoon kosher salt
- ½ cup (113 grams) cold unsalted butter, cubed
- 4 to 6 tablespoons (60 to 90 grams) ice water
- 1 large egg (50 grams), lightly beaten

1. In a large bowl, whisk together flour, sugar, and salt. Using a pastry blender or 2 forks, cut in cold butter until mixture is crumbly. Using a fork, stir in 4 tablespoons (60 grams) ice water until a shaggy dough forms; add up to remaining 2 tablespoons (30 grams) ice water, 1 tablespoon (15 grams) at a time, if necessary.

2. Turn out dough onto a lightly floured surface, and shape into a disk. Wrap tightly in plastic wrap, and refrigerate for at least 1 hour or up to 2 days.

3. Preheat oven to 400°F (200°C).

4. Let dough stand at room temperature until slightly softened, about 10 minutes. On a lightly floured surface, roll dough into a 12-inch circle. Transfer to a 9-inch pie plate, pressing into bottom and up sides. Fold edges under, and crimp, if desired. Freeze for 20 minutes.

5. Brush edges of dough with egg. Place pan on a rimmed baking sheet. Top with a piece of parchment paper, letting ends extend over edges of plate. Add pie weights.

6. Bake until golden brown, about 25 minutes. Carefully remove parchment and weights. Let cool completely.

IN-FLIGHT PIE

Makes 1 (9-inch) pie

Inspired by my former days as a flight attendant, this pie has all the recognizable flavors of an in-flight snack service—rich coffee, nutty peanuts, and irresistible Biscoff cookies. Originating in Belgium in 1932, Biscoff cookies were first known as Europe's "favorite cookie with coffee" before becoming the treat many Americans associate with air travel. Made from these crushed cookies of airline fame and other tasty ingredients, Biscoff spread has an amazingly rich flavor that takes this no-bake pie to new heights. Please sit back, relax, and enjoy this airline-inspired delight.

1   (8.8-ounce) package (250 grams) speculaas cookies*
6   tablespoons (84 grams) unsalted butter, melted
¼   teaspoon kosher salt
1   cup (240 grams) creamy cookie butter*
½   cup (120 grams) heavy whipping cream, divided
¼   cup (50 grams) granulated sugar
¼   cup (14 grams) instant espresso powder
8   ounces (226 grams) cream cheese, softened
1   cup (104 grams) marshmallow crème*
Garnish: sweetened whipped cream, crushed speculaas cookies, chopped roasted salted peanuts

1. In the work bowl of a food processor, pulse cookies until finely ground. Transfer to a medium bowl; stir in melted butter and salt. Using a measuring cup, press mixture into bottom and up sides of a 9-inch pie plate. Freeze until firm, about 15 minutes.
2. Spoon cookie butter into bottom of prepared crust. Freeze for 15 minutes.
3. In a small microwave-safe bowl, heat ¼ cup (60 grams) cream on high until hot, 25 to 30 seconds. Stir in sugar and espresso powder until dissolved. Freeze until cold, about 15 minutes.
4. In another medium bowl, beat espresso mixture and remaining ¼ cup (60 grams) cream with a mixer at medium speed until soft peaks form.
5. In a large bowl, beat cream cheese and marshmallow crème with a mixer at medium speed until smooth. Fold in espresso mixture. Spoon into prepared crust, smoothing top with an offset spatula.
6. Refrigerate until firm, about 3 hours or up to 3 days. Garnish with sweetened whipped cream, crushed cookies, and peanuts, if desired.

We used Biscoff Cookies, Biscoff Cookie Butter, and Jet-Puffed Marshmallow Crème.

SILKY CHOCOLATE TART

Makes 1 (9-inch) tart

Inspired by French silk pie, this tangy tart receives a triple boost of cream cheese in its crust, filling, and whipped topping.

Crust:
½ cup (113 grams) unsalted butter, softened
⅓ cup plus 2 teaspoons (85 grams) cream cheese, softened
1 cup (125 grams) all-purpose flour
½ teaspoon (1.5 grams) kosher salt

Filling:
¼ cup (50 grams) granulated sugar
¼ cup (55 grams) firmly packed light brown sugar
2 large eggs (100 grams)
2.5 ounces (71 grams) 64% cacao semisweet chocolate baking bars, finely chopped
1 teaspoon (2 grams) instant espresso powder
¼ teaspoon kosher salt
¼ cup (57 grams) unsalted butter, softened
¼ cup (56 grams) cream cheese, softened
1¼ cups (300 grams) cold heavy whipping cream
1 tablespoon (20 grams) coffee liqueur*

Topping:
3 ounces (86 grams) cream cheese, softened
⅓ cup (67 grams) granulated sugar
1 cup (240 grams) cold heavy whipping cream

Garnish: chocolate shavings

1. For crust: In the bowl of a stand mixer fitted with the paddle attachment, beat butter and cream cheese at medium speed until smooth. With mixer on low speed, gradually add flour and salt, beating until combined. Turn out dough onto a lightly floured surface, and shape into a disk. Wrap in plastic wrap, and refrigerate for at least 1 hour.

2. Preheat oven to 350°F (180°C). Lightly spray a 1-inch-tall 9½-inch fluted round removable-bottom tart pan with cooking spray.

3. Let dough stand at room temperature until slightly softened, about 10 minutes. On a lightly floured surface, roll dough into a 12- to 13-inch circle (about ⅛ inch thick). Transfer to prepared pan, pressing into bottom and up sides. Trim excess dough. Using a fork, prick bottom and sides of dough. Freeze until firm, about 15 minutes.

4. Lightly spray a piece of parchment paper with cooking spray; top dough with parchment, spray side down, letting ends extend over edges of pan. Add pie weights.

5. Bake until edges are lightly golden and set, about 20 minutes. Carefully remove parchment and weights. Bake until crust is golden brown, 10 to 15 minutes more, pricking bottom and sides with a fork again and gently pressing down center of crust if needed. (It's OK if crust shrinks slightly in pan.) Let cool completely in pan on a wire rack.

6. For filling: In the top of a double boiler, whisk together sugars and eggs. Cook over simmering water, stirring frequently, until mixture is thick enough to coat the back of a spoon and an instant-read thermometer registers 160°F (71°C), 5 to 10 minutes. Add chocolate, espresso powder, and salt, stirring until smooth and well combined. Remove from heat; let cool for 10 minutes.

7. Meanwhile, in the bowl of a stand mixer fitted with the paddle attachment, beat butter at medium speed until creamy, 30 seconds to 1 minute, stopping to scrape sides of bowl. Add cream cheese; beat until smooth and well combined, about 30 seconds, stopping to scrape sides of bowl. Beat in cooled chocolate mixture until well combined, stopping to scrape sides of bowl. Transfer mixture to a large bowl.

8. Clean bowl of stand mixer. Using the whisk attachment, beat cream and liqueur at medium-high speed until stiff peaks form, 2 to 3 minutes. Fold cream mixture into chocolate mixture in three additions until smooth and well combined; spoon into prepared crust, piling high; spread and swirl with an offset spatula or the back of a spoon as desired.

9. For topping: Clean bowl of stand mixer and whisk attachment. Beat cream cheese and sugar at medium speed until smooth and well combined, about 1 minute, stopping to scrape sides of bowl. Reduce mixer speed to medium-low; slowly beat in one-third of cold cream until smooth, stopping frequently to scrape sides of bowl. Increase mixer speed to medium, and gradually add remaining cold cream, beating until stiff peaks form, 2 to 4 minutes. (Do not overprocess.) Spread and swirl topping on tart as desired. Refrigerate for at least 4 hours or overnight. Just before serving, garnish with chocolate shavings, if desired.

We used Kahlúa.

EGGNOG CUSTARD TART

Makes 1 (9-inch) tart

Browned Butter lends nutty depth to the shortbread crust of this indulgent dessert. A dash of spiced rum gives the creamy eggnog custard a little kick. We'd remind you this is best enjoyed the same day, but you won't be able to resist having a slice (or two or three) once it's out of the oven anyway.

Browned Butter (recipe follows), softened
⅓   cup (40 grams) confectioners' sugar
¾   teaspoon (3 grams) vanilla extract
½   teaspoon (1.5 grams) kosher salt
1½ cups (188 grams) all-purpose flour
Eggnog Custard Filling (recipe follows)
Grated fresh nutmeg and grated fresh cinnamon, for dusting
Garnish: white chocolate curls (see Note)

1. In the bowl of a stand mixer fitted with the paddle attachment, beat Browned Butter at low speed until smooth, about 1 minute. Add confectioners' sugar, vanilla, and salt, beating until combined, stopping to scrape sides of bowl. Gradually add flour, beating until combined and dough comes together, 3 to 4 minutes.
2. Press dough into a 9-inch fluted round removable-bottom tart pan. Gently press dough into bottom and up sides of pan until smooth and even. Freeze for 30 minutes.
3. Preheat oven to 350°F (180°C). Line a baking sheet with parchment paper.
4. Remove tart pan from freezer. Place tart pan on prepared baking sheet.
5. Bake until light golden brown around the edges, 15 to 20 minutes. While crust is still warm, gently flatten any puffed areas with the back of a spoon. Let cool completely on a wire rack.
6. Pour warm Eggnog Custard Filling into prepared crust. Generously dust with nutmeg and cinnamon.
7. Bake until set around the edges but still slightly jiggly in center, 25 to 30 minutes. Let cool completely on a wire rack. Garnish with white chocolate curls, if desired. This tart is best enjoyed the day it is baked.

Note: *To create white chocolate curls, use a vegetable peeler to shave off thin pieces of a room temperature block of white chocolate. We used Callebaut White Chocolate.*

Browned Butter
Makes ¾ cup

¾   cup (170 grams) unsalted butter

1. In a medium saucepan, melt butter over medium heat. Cook, stirring constantly, until butter turns a medium-brown color and has a nutty aroma, 7 to 10 minutes. Immediately transfer to a small bowl; let cool completely. Refrigerate until ready to use.

Eggnog Custard Filling
Makes 2 cups

1   cup (240 grams) half-and-half
½   cup (120 grams) whole milk
1   tablespoon (15 grams) dark spiced rum
2   teaspoons (8 grams) vanilla extract
6   large egg yolks (112 grams)
⅓   cup (67 grams) castor sugar (see Note)

1. In a medium saucepan, heat half-and-half, milk, rum, and vanilla over medium heat, stirring frequently, just until bubbles form around edges of pan. (Do not boil.) Remove from heat.
2. In a medium bowl, whisk together egg yolks and sugar. Slowly pour in hot milk mixture, whisking constantly. Strain mixture through a fine-mesh sieve. Use immediately.

Note: *To make castor sugar, in the container of a blender or the work bowl of a food processor, blend or pulse ⅓ cup (67 grams) granulated sugar in short bursts, 2 to 3 times, until sugar becomes superfine. If sugar reaches a powdery consistency, you've gone too far.*

BUTTERSCOTCH PIE WITH COCONUT CURRY CRUST

Makes 1 (9-inch) pie

A bit of curry in the crust pairs perfectly with the custardy butterscotch filling in this sweet yet slightly savory dessert.

½ cup (113 grams) unsalted butter, cubed
1¾ cups (385 grams) firmly packed dark brown sugar
¾ teaspoon (2.25 grams) kosher salt
⅔ cup (160 grams) heavy whipping cream, room temperature
4 large eggs (200 grams)
2 large egg yolks (37 grams)
1 tablespoon (13 grams) vanilla extract
Coconut Curry Crust (recipe follows)
Garnish: confectioners' sugar

1. Preheat oven to 400°F (200°C).
2. In a medium saucepan, melt butter over medium heat. Add brown sugar and salt, stirring until combined. Bring to a simmer, and cook for 3 minutes, stirring constantly. Remove from heat, and carefully whisk in cream. Let cool for 20 minutes.
3. To cream mixture, add eggs and egg yolks, one at a time, whisking until well combined after each addition. Stir in vanilla. Pour into prepared Coconut Curry Crust.
4. Bake for 10 minutes. Reduce oven temperature to 300°F (150°C), and bake until set but slightly jiggly in center, 25 to 30 minutes more. Let cool completely. Garnish with confectioners' sugar, if desired. Cover and refrigerate for up to 5 days.

COCONUT CURRY CRUST

Makes 1 (9-inch) crust

1¼ cups (156 grams) all-purpose flour
¼ cup (21 grams) desiccated coconut, toasted
1½ teaspoons (6 grams) granulated sugar
1 teaspoon (2 grams) Madras curry powder
½ teaspoon (1 gram) ground ginger
½ teaspoon (1.5 grams) kosher salt
½ teaspoon (1 gram) ground black pepper
¼ teaspoon ground turmeric
½ cup (113 grams) cold unsalted butter, cubed
¼ cup (60 grams) ice water

1. In the work bowl of a food processor, place flour, coconut, sugar, curry powder, ginger, salt, pepper, and turmeric; pulse until combined. Add cold butter, and pulse until mixture is crumbly. Add ¼ cup (60 grams) ice water,, 1 tablespoon (15 grams) at a time, just until dough comes together. Turn out dough, and shape into a disk. Wrap tightly in plastic wrap, and refrigerate for at least 30 minutes. Dough may be refrigerated for up to 3 days or frozen for up to 2 months.
2. On a lightly floured surface, roll dough into a 12-inch circle. Transfer to a 9-inch pie plate, pressing into bottom and up sides. Trim excess dough to ½ inch beyond edge of plate. Fold edges under. Using kitchen scissors, make a ¼-inch-thick (45-degree) cut into dough, being careful not to cut all the way through dough. Lay dough piece over to left side. Make another ¼-inch-thick cut, and lay to right side. Repeat procedure around pie until you reach first cut. Freeze for 20 minutes.
3. Preheat oven to 400°F (200°C).
4. Top dough with a piece of parchment paper, letting ends extend over edges of plate. Add pie weights.
5. Bake for 20 minutes. Carefully remove parchment and weights. Let cool completely.

CLASSIC
COMBOS

FROM FRESH FRUIT PIES THAT HIGHLIGHT EACH
GROWING SEASON TO RECIPES PACKED WITH BUTTERY
PECANS AND RICH CHOCOLATE, THESE RECIPES HAVE
ACHIEVED ICON STATUS FOR A REASON

STEPHEN'S BUTTERMILK PIE

Makes 1 (9-inch) pie

It wouldn't be a proper holiday celebration without my husband's favorite buttermilk pie—a recipe his grandmother made for special occasions. While I'm the baker in our family, I happily step aside for Stephen to bake this one. Rather unassuming, this classic uses simple pantry staples, but it is anything but ordinary. The rich filling sets up to a brilliant custard in the oven, caramelizing the top and creating a characteristic sugary crust with undeniable crunch. Enveloped in a flaky, buttery crust, this pie is not one to miss.

Pie Dough (recipe follows)
1½   cups (300 grams) granulated sugar
3   tablespoons (24 grams) all-purpose flour, sifted
6   tablespoons (84 grams) butter, melted and cooled to room temperature
3   large eggs (150 grams), room temperature
1½   teaspoons (6 grams) vanilla extract
¾   cup (180 grams) whole buttermilk, room temperature

1. Preheat oven to 400°F (200°C).
2. Let Pie Dough stand at room temperature until softened, 10 to 15 minutes. On a lightly floured surface, roll dough into a 12-inch circle. Transfer to a 9-inch pie plate, pressing into bottom and up sides. Trim excess dough to ½ inch beyond edge of pan. Fold edges under, and crimp, if desired. Freeze for 15 minutes.
3. Top Pie Dough with a piece of parchment paper, letting ends extend over edges of pan. Add pie weights.
4. Bake until edges are just dry, 10 to 15 minutes. Carefully remove parchment and weights. Bake until bottom is dry and set, 2 to 5 minutes more, lightly covering edges with foil to prevent excess browning, if necessary. (Crust may puff up some, but this is normal.) Let cool completely on a wire rack, at least 20 minutes. Reduce oven temperature to 325°F (170°C).
5. In the bowl of a stand mixer fitted with a paddle attachment, beat sugar and flour at low speed until combined. Add melted butter, eggs, and vanilla, and beat at medium speed until well combined. Add buttermilk, and beat at low speed just until combined. Pour into prepared crust.

6. Bake until center is set, top is lightly golden brown, a knife inserted in center comes out clean, and an instant-read thermometer inserted in center registers 200°F (93°C), about 1 hour, covering edges with foil to prevent excess browning, if necessary. (Pie will be puffed when removed from oven but will sink slightly while cooling.) Let cool completely before refrigerating.

PIE DOUGH

Makes 1 (9-inch) crust

1½   cups (188 grams) all-purpose flour
1   teaspoon (3 grams) kosher salt
½   cup (113 grams) cold unsalted butter, cubed
4 to 5 tablespoons (60 to 75 grams) ice water

1. In the work bowl of a food processor, place flour and salt; pulse until combined. Add cold butter, and pulse until mixture is crumbly and butter is pea-size. With processor running, add 4 tablespoons (60 grams) ice water in a slow, steady stream just until dough comes together; add up to remaining 1 tablespoon (15 grams) water, 1 teaspoon (5 grams) at a time, if necessary. (Mixture may appear crumbly. It should be moist and hold together when pinched.)
2. Turn out dough, and shape into a disk. Wrap tightly in plastic wrap, and refrigerate for at least 1 hour. Dough may be refrigerated for up to 3 days or frozen for up to 2 months.

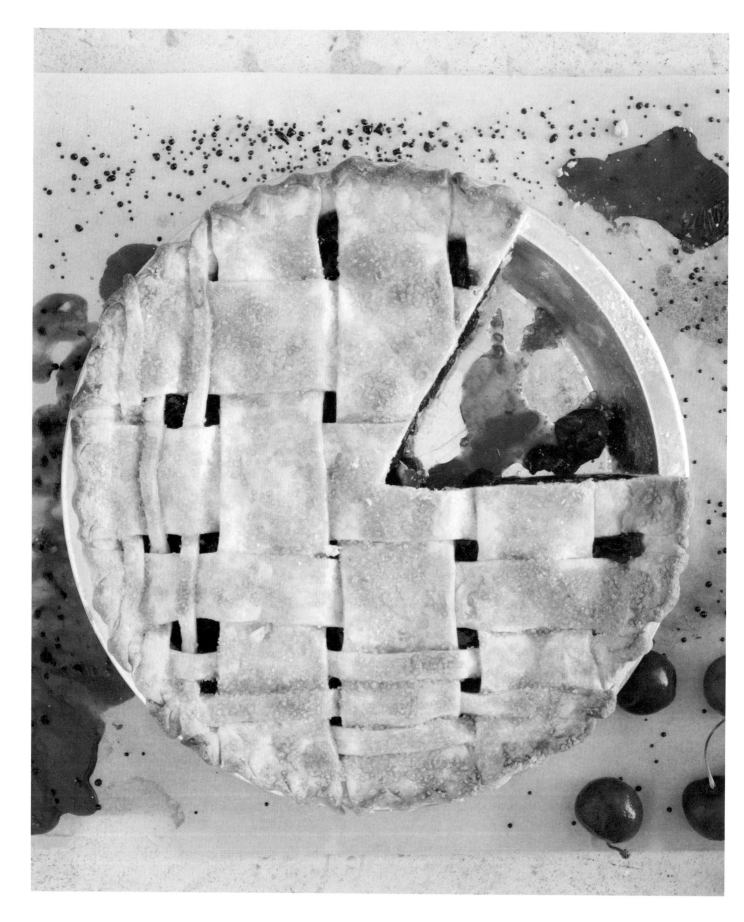

CHERRY PIE

Makes 1 (9-inch) pie

Nothing compares to fresh cherry pie. This recipe is simple and classic, sure to become a staple on your summer to do list.

2   pounds (907 grams) fresh sweet cherries, pitted
⅔   cup (133 grams) granulated sugar
½   cup (120 grams) water
¼   cup (32 grams) cornstarch
2   tablespoons (30 grams) fresh lemon juice
1   vanilla bean, split lengthwise, seeds scraped and reserved
Our Favorite Piecrust (recipe follows)
1   large egg (50 grams), lightly beaten
2   tablespoons (24 grams) turbinado sugar

1. In a medium saucepan, combine cherries, granulated sugar, ½ cup (120 grams) water, cornstarch, lemon juice, and reserved vanilla bean seeds. Bring to a boil over medium-high heat. Reduce heat to low, and cook, stirring frequently, being careful not to crush cherries, until thickened, about 10 minutes. Remove from heat, and let cool.
2. Preheat oven to 375°F (190°C).
3. Let Our Favorite Piecrust stand at room temperature until slightly softened, about 5 minutes. On a lightly floured surface, roll half of dough into a 12-inch circle. Transfer to a 9-inch pie plate, pressing into bottom and up sides. Trim excess dough to ½ inch beyond edge of plate. Spoon filling into prepared crust.
4. On a lightly floured surface, roll remaining dough into a 12-inch circle. Cut dough into strips of varying widths. Arrange dough strips on pie in a lattice design. Trim dough strips, fold edges under, and crimp, if desired. Brush dough with egg, and sprinkle with turbinado sugar. Place on a baking sheet.
5. Bake until golden brown and bubbly, 40 to 50 minutes. Let cool for at least 2 hours before serving.

Our Favorite Piecrust
Makes 1 (9-inch) double crust

2¾   cups (344 grams) all-purpose flour
2   tablespoons (24 grams) granulated sugar
2   teaspoons (6 grams) kosher salt
1   cup (227 grams) cold unsalted butter, cubed
6 to 10 tablespoons (90 to 150 grams) ice water

1. In the work bowl of a food processor, place flour, sugar, and salt; pulse until combined. Add cold butter, and pulse until mixture is crumbly. Add 6 to 10 tablespoons (90 to 150 grams) ice water, 1 tablespoon (15 grams) at a time, just until dough comes together.
2. Divide dough in half, and shape each half into a disk. Wrap tightly in plastic wrap, and refrigerate for at least 2 hours. Dough may be refrigerated for up to 3 days or frozen for up to 2 months.

HONEY NUT PIE

Makes 1 (9-inch) pie

If you like a pie with some crunch, this is the recipe for you. This remix on the classic pecan pie abounds with texture. Smooth orange blossom honey and a tender Pâte Brisée crust soften the unique blend of pine nuts, hazelnuts, pecans, and walnuts.

Pâte Brisée (recipe follows)
½   cup (100 grams) granulated sugar
⅓   cup (113 grams) orange blossom honey
¼   cup (85 grams) light corn syrup
1   teaspoon (3 grams) kosher salt
¾   cup (170 grams) unsalted butter, cubed
½   cup (120 grams) heavy whipping cream
1   large egg (50 grams)
1   large egg yolk (19 grams)
½   cup (57 grams) pine nuts
½   cup (57 grams) chopped pecans
½   cup (57 grams) chopped walnuts
½   cup (57 grams) chopped hazelnuts, toasted and skins removed

1. On a lightly floured surface, roll Pâte Brisée into a 12-inch circle. Transfer to a 9-inch pie plate, pressing into bottom and up sides. Trim excess dough to ½ inch beyond edge of plate. Fold edges under, and crimp as desired. Freeze for 20 minutes.
2. Preheat oven to 350°F (180°C).
3. Top dough with a piece of parchment paper, letting ends extend over edges of plate. Add pie weights.
4. Bake until edges are set and golden brown, about 12 minutes. Carefully remove paper and weights. Bake 8 minutes more. Let cool completely.
5. In a medium saucepan, bring sugar, honey, corn syrup, and salt to a boil over medium heat, stirring until sugar is dissolved. Add butter, whisking to combine. Transfer to a medium bowl, and let cool for 30 minutes.
6. Whisk cream, egg, and egg yolk into honey mixture. Arrange nuts in bottom of prepared crust. Pour honey mixture over nuts.
7. Bake until crust is golden brown and center is set, 50 minutes to 1 hour, covering crust with foil to prevent excess browning, if necessary. Let cool completely on a wire rack.

PÂTE BRISÉE
Makes 1 (9-inch) crust

Because of its mixing method and smaller amount of sugar, Pâte Brisée is sturdier and easier to handle than other forms of shortcrust, like Pâte Sucrée, which makes it perfect for pies.

1½   cups (188 grams) all-purpose flour
1½   teaspoons (6 grams) granulated sugar
½   teaspoon (1.5 grams) kosher salt
½   cup (113 grams) cold unsalted butter, cubed
¼   cup (60 grams) ice water

1. In the bowl of a stand mixer fitted with the paddle attachment, beat flour, sugar, and salt at low speed until combined. Increase mixer speed to medium-low. Add cold butter, and beat until mixture is crumbly. With mixer running, add ¼ cup (60 grams) ice water, beating until dough comes together. Turn out dough, and shape into a disk. Wrap tightly in plastic wrap, and refrigerate for at least 30 minutes. Dough may be refrigerated for up to 3 days or frozen for up to 2 months.

Note: *Chilling the Pâte Brisée dough is crucial. The butter needs to stay cold, and the flour needs time to fully absorb water before it's rolled out. If you choose to refrigerate the dough for longer than the required 30 minutes, let it warm up on the counter for 10 minutes before rolling it out.*

APPLE CHEDDAR PIE

Makes 1 (9-inch) pie

For this modern twist on traditional apple pie, two piecrusts are used, a Traditional American Piecrust and a Cheddar Cheese Piecrust, to create a marbled look.

Traditional American Piecrust (on opposite page)
Cheddar Cheese Piecrust (recipe follows)

8	cups (884 grams) ¼-inch-sliced peeled Granny Smith apples*
⅓	cup (73 grams) firmly packed light brown sugar
2	tablespoons (16 grams) all-purpose flour
1	teaspoon (2 grams) lemon zest
2	tablespoons (30 grams) fresh lemon juice
1	teaspoon (2 grams) ground black pepper
½	teaspoon (1.5 grams) kosher salt
¼	teaspoon ground nutmeg
¼	teaspoon ground cinnamon
1	large egg (50 grams)
1	tablespoon (15 grams) heavy whipping cream
1	tablespoon (12 grams) turbinado sugar

1. Preheat oven to 375°F (190°C).
2. On a lightly floured surface, roll Traditional American Piecrust into an 18x3-inch rectangle. Repeat procedure with Cheddar Cheese Piecrust. Place Traditional American Piecrust on top of Cheddar Cheese Piecrust. Starting with one long side, roll into a log, jelly-roll style, and pinch seam to seal. Wrap in plastic wrap, and refrigerate for 20 minutes.
3. On a lightly floured surface, cut dough crosswise into 2 (1½-inch-long) logs. Stand up logs vertically. Roll half of dough into a 12-inch circle. Transfer to a 9-inch pie plate, pressing into bottom and up sides. Trim excess dough to ½ inch beyond edge of plate.
4. In a large bowl, combine apple slices, brown sugar, flour, lemon zest and juice, pepper, salt, nutmeg, and cinnamon. Spoon apple mixture into prepared crust.
5. Roll remaining dough into a 12-inch square. Cut into 6 (2-inch-wide) strips. Place 3 dough strips vertically on pie, spacing evenly apart. Fold back alternating strips, and place one dough strip horizontally across

vertical strips; unfold folded strips. Fold back center vertical strip, and place another horizontal strip across first strips, spacing evenly. Unfold vertical folded strip, then fold back alternating vertical strips. Place another horizontal strip across vertical strip, spacing evenly. Unfold vertical folded strips.
6. Trim lattice until it meets inside of pan's lip. Roll excess dough from crust over so that it is even with inside lip of pan, pressing down to make it adhere. Crimp as desired.
7. In a small bowl, whisk together egg and cream. Brush dough with egg wash. Sprinkle with turbinado sugar.
8. Bake until crust is golden brown and filling is bubbly, about 1 hour, covering with foil to prevent excess browning, if necessary. Let cool slightly; serve warm.

While we prefer to use Granny Smith, it's fine to combine three to four kinds of apples in an apple pie. Be sure to use ones with low water content, such as Macoun, Cortland, Golden Delicious, York Imperial, or Pink Lady.

CHEDDAR CHEESE PIECRUST
Makes 1 (9-inch) crust

1¼	cups (156 grams) all-purpose flour
½	teaspoon (1.5 grams) kosher salt
½	teaspoon (1 gram) dry mustard
½	teaspoon (1 gram) smoked paprika
1	cup (100 grams) freshly grated extra-sharp Cheddar cheese
¼	cup (57 grams) cold unsalted butter, cubed
¼	cup (60 grams) ice water

1. In the work bowl of a food processor, place flour, salt, dry mustard, and paprika; pulse until combined. Add Cheddar and cold butter, and pulse until mixture is crumbly. With processor running, pour ¼ cup (60 grams) ice water through food chute in a slow, steady stream just until dough comes together. (Mixture may appear crumbly. It should be moist and hold together when pinched.) Turn out dough, and shape into a disk. Wrap tightly in plastic wrap, and refrigerate for at least 30 minutes. Dough may be refrigerated for up to 3 days or frozen for up to 2 months.

TRADITIONAL AMERICAN PIECRUST

Makes 1 (9-inch) crust

Meet your new go-to pie dough. This crust's paper-thin layers will melt in your mouth while effortlessly holding the heaviest of fruit fillings. Its easy-to-handle dough makes it great for lattice designs.

1½   **cups (188 grams) all-purpose flour**
½   **teaspoon (1.5 grams) kosher salt**
½   **cup (113 grams) cold unsalted butter, cubed**
⅓   **cup (80 grams) ice water**

1. In the work bowl of a food processor, place flour and salt; pulse until combined. Add cold butter, and pulse until mixture is crumbly. With processor running, pour ⅓ cup (80 grams) ice water through food chute in a slow, steady stream just until dough comes together. (Mixture may appear crumbly. It should be moist and hold together when pinched.) Turn out dough, and shape into a disk. Wrap tightly in plastic wrap, and refrigerate for at least 30 minutes. Dough may be refrigerated for up to 3 days or frozen for up to 2 months.

Note: *Press the dough into a disk rather than shaping it into a ball to allow it to chill faster. This will also make the dough easier to roll out.*

HOMESTYLE BERRY PIE

Makes 1 (9-inch) pie

Loaded with fresh berries, this pie gets a touch of warmth from cardamom in the filling. As for that buttery crust—there's no butter. Lard is added to give the crust a tender, melt-in-your-mouth texture (but you can also substitute unsalted butter, if you prefer).

Pie Dough (recipe follows)
1   pound (454 grams) fresh blackberries (about 3 cups)
1   pound (454 grams) fresh blueberries (about 3 cups)
¾   cup (150 grams) plus 2 teaspoons (8 grams) granulated sugar, divided
⅓   cup (43 grams) cornstarch
1   teaspoon (2 grams) ground cardamom
⅛   teaspoon kosher salt
1   large egg (50 grams)
1   tablespoon (15 grams) water
Vanilla ice cream, to serve

1. On a lightly floured surface, roll half of Pie Dough into a 12-inch circle. Transfer to a 9-inch pie plate, pressing into bottom and up sides. Refrigerate until ready to use. On a lightly floured surface, roll remaining Pie Dough into a 12-inch circle. Place on a parchment paper-lined baking sheet, and refrigerate for at least 10 minutes.
2. In a large bowl, toss together blackberries, blueberries, ¾ cup (150 grams) sugar, cornstarch, cardamom, and salt. Spoon filling into prepared crust. Place remaining dough over filling. Trim excess dough; fold edges under. Working your way around edge, gently pinch crust with thumb and knuckle of forefinger to create crimps. Cut several 1-inch vents in top of dough to release steam. Freeze for 30 minutes.
3. Preheat oven to 425°F (220°C). Line a baking sheet with parchment paper.
4. In a small bowl, whisk together egg and 1 tablespoon (15 grams) water. Place pie on prepared pan, and brush top with egg wash. Sprinkle with remaining 2 teaspoons (8 grams) sugar.
5. Bake for 30 minutes. Reduce oven temperature to 350°F (180°C). Loosely cover with foil, and bake until crust is lightly browned and filling is bubbly, about 1 hour and 10 minutes more. Let cool on a wire rack. Serve warm with ice cream.

PIE DOUGH

Makes 1 (9-inch) double crust

3   cups (375 grams) all-purpose flour
2   tablespoons (24 grams) granulated sugar
½   teaspoon (1.5 grams) kosher salt
1   cup (227 grams) cold lard, cubed
5 to 7 tablespoons (75 to 105 grams) ice water

1. In the work bowl of a food processor, pulse together flour, sugar, and salt until combined. Add cold lard, and pulse until mixture is crumbly. With processor running, add 5 tablespoons (75 grams) ice water in a slow, steady stream until combined and dough comes together; add up to remaining 2 tablespoons (30 grams) ice water, 1 tablespoon (15 grams) at a time, if needed. Turn out dough, and divide in half. Shape each half into a disk, and wrap in plastic wrap. Refrigerate for at least 30 minutes.

STRAWBERRIES & CREAM PIE

Makes 1 (9-inch) pie

Double-crusted and jam-packed with strawberries, this pie is delicious with a generous scoop of freshly whipped cream.

Pie Dough (recipe follows), divided
6   cups (882 grams) ½-inch-diced fresh strawberries
½   cup (100 grams) granulated sugar
½   cup (60 grams) tapioca flour
2   teaspoons (2 grams) lemon zest
1   tablespoon (15 grams) lemon juice
2   teaspoons (12 grams) vanilla bean paste
1   large egg (50 grams)
1   tablespoon (15 grams) water
Sparkling sugar, for sprinkling
Vanilla Whipped Cream (recipe follows)
Garnish: halved fresh strawberries

1. Preheat oven to 425°F (220°C). Spray a 9-inch pie plate with baking spray with flour.
2. On a lightly floured surface, roll half of Pie Dough into a 12-inch circle. Transfer to prepared plate, pressing into bottom and up sides. Trim edges to ¼ inch past rim of plate, if necessary.
3. In a large bowl, toss together strawberries, granulated sugar, flour, lemon zest and juice, and vanilla bean paste. Let stand for 10 minutes, stirring occasionally. Pour into prepared crust.
4. On a lightly floured surface, roll remaining Pie Dough into a 12-inch circle. Cut into 1-inch-wide strips. Place 6 dough strips horizontally on pie, spacing evenly apart. Fold back alternating strips, and place 1 dough strip vertically across horizontal strips; unfold folded strips. Fold back alternating horizontal strips, and place another vertical strip across first strips, spacing evenly. Unfold horizontal folded strips and then fold back alternating horizontal strips. Place another vertical strip across first strips, spacing evenly. Unfold horizontal folded strips. Repeat with remaining vertical strips. Press strips into bottom crust, and trim strips even with bottom crust. Fold edges under, and crimp, if desired. Freeze for 10 minutes.
5. In a small bowl, whisk together egg and 1 tablespoon (15 grams) water until smooth. Brush onto prepared crust. Sprinkle with sparkling sugar. Place pie on a parchment-lined baking sheet.
6. Bake for 15 minutes. Reduce oven temperature to 350°F (180°C), and bake until filling is bubbly in center, 1 hour and 30 minutes to 1 hour and 35 minutes, covering with foil after 30 minutes of baking to prevent excess browning. Let cool completely before serving. Serve with Vanilla Whipped Cream. Garnish with halved strawberries, if desired.

PIE DOUGH
Makes 1 (9-inch) double crust

3   cups (375 grams) all-purpose flour
2   tablespoons (24 grams) granulated sugar
1½   teaspoons (4.5 grams) kosher salt
1   cup (227 grams) cold unsalted butter, cubed
8 to 9 tablespoons (120 to 135 grams) ice water

1. In the work bowl of a food processor, pulse together flour, sugar, and salt until combined. Add cold butter, and pulse until mixture is crumbly. With processor running, add 8 tablespoons (120 grams) ice water in a slow, steady stream just until dough comes together. (Mixture may appear crumbly. It should be moist and hold together when pinched. Add remaining 1 tablespoon [15 grams] ice water, if needed.)
2. Turn out dough; divide in half (about 386 grams each), and shape into disks. Wrap tightly in plastic wrap, and refrigerate for at least 30 minutes. Dough can be refrigerated for up to 3 days or frozen for up to 2 months.

VANILLA WHIPPED CREAM
Makes about 1 cup

½   cup (120 grams) cold heavy whipping cream
1   tablespoon (12 grams) granulated sugar
½   teaspoon (3 grams) vanilla bean paste

1. In a medium bowl, whisk together all ingredients until soft to medium peaks form. Refrigerate until ready to use.

FRENCH COCONUT PIE

Makes 1 (9-inch) pie

From the tangy buttermilk pie dough base to the toasted coconut crust, this pie takes the classic chess pie formula and turns the flavor up to 11. This one's for you, coconut lovers.

Buttermilk Pie Dough (recipe follows)
1½ cups (300 grams) granulated sugar
3   tablespoons (24 grams) all-purpose flour
¼   teaspoon kosher salt
3   large eggs (150 grams), room temperature
6   tablespoons (84 grams) unsalted butter, melted and cooled slightly
1½ teaspoons (9 grams) vanilla bean paste
¼   teaspoon (1 gram) coconut extract
¾   cup (180 grams) whole buttermilk, room temperature
2   cups (200 grams) sweetened flaked coconut
Buttermilk Whipped Cream (recipe follows)
Garnish: lightly toasted sweetened flaked coconut if desired

1. Position oven rack in bottom third of oven. Preheat oven to 400°F (200°C).
2. On a lightly floured surface, roll Buttermilk Pie Dough into a 12-inch circle (about ⅛ inch thick). Transfer to a 9-inch pie plate, pressing into bottom and up sides. Trim excess dough to ½ inch beyond edge of pan, if needed. Fold edges under, and crimp, if desired. (See PRO TIP.). Freeze for 15 minutes.
3. In a large bowl, whisk together sugar, flour, and salt. Whisk in eggs, melted butter, vanilla bean paste, and coconut extract until combined. Slowly add buttermilk, whisking until just combined. Stir in flaked coconut. Pour into prepared crust.
4. Bake for 15 minutes. Reduce oven temperature to 325°F (170°C), and bake until the edges are set but the center still has a slight jiggle, and an instant-read thermometer inserted in center registers 200°F (93°C), about 35 minutes. An instant-read thermometer inserted in the center will register 200°F (93°C). (Pie will be puffed at first and then deflate slightly as it cools.) Let cool completely on a wire rack. Refrigerate until ready to serve. Serve cold or at room temperature with Buttermilk Whipped Cream. Garnish with toasted coconut, if desired.

> **PRO TIP**
> For a braided edge, roll dough scraps into a 12x6-inch rectangle. Cut 6 (¼-inch) strips, and divide into two groups of three; weave into two braids. Whisk 1 egg (50 grams). Brush edges of prepared crust with egg wash, and place dough braids on edge, allowing braids to meet on either end.

BUTTERMILK PIE DOUGH
Makes 1 (9-inch) crust

1½ cups (188 grams) all-purpose flour
1   teaspoon (3 grams) kosher salt
½   cup (113 grams) cold unsalted butter, cubed
4 to 5 tablespoons (60 to 75 grams) cold whole buttermilk

1. In the work bowl of a food processor, place flour and salt; pulse until combined. Add cold butter, and pulse until mixture is crumbly and butter is pea-size. With processor running, add 4 tablespoons (60 grams) cold buttermilk in a slow, steady stream just until dough comes together; add up to remaining 1 tablespoon (15 grams) cold buttermilk, 1 teaspoon (5 grams) at a time, if needed. (Mixture may appear crumbly. It should be moist and hold together when pinched.) Add additional 1 tablespoon (15 grams) of buttermilk only if needed. Turn out dough, and shape into a disk. Wrap tightly in plastic wrap, and refrigerate for at least 30 minutes. Dough may be refrigerated for up to 3 days or frozen for up to 2 months.

BUTTERMILK WHIPPED CREAM
Makes about 2 cups

¾   cup (180 grams) cold heavy whipping cream
¼   cup (60 grams) cold whole buttermilk
3   tablespoons (36 grams) granulated sugar

1. In a large bowl, whisk together all ingredients until thickened and reaches medium-stiff.

PUMPKIN PIE WITH WHIPPED CREAM

Makes 1 (9-inch) pie

Our fabulous traditional pumpkin pie is topped with pillowy Whipped Cream and decorative fall cutouts. A light dusting of cinnamon adds the perfect final touch, accentuating the flavors of the silky pumpkin custard filling.

Pie Dough (recipe follows)
5 eggs (250 grams), room temperature and divided
1 teaspoon (5 grams) water
2⅓ cups (569 grams) canned pumpkin
1⅓ cups (320 grams) evaporated milk
⅔ cup (133 grams) granulated sugar
⅓ cup (73 grams) firmly packed light brown sugar
⅓ cup (76 grams) unsalted butter, melted
1½ teaspoons (6 grams) vanilla extract
3 tablespoons (24 grams) all-purpose flour*
1½ teaspoons (3 grams) ground cinnamon
1 teaspoon (2 grams) ground ginger
¾ teaspoon (2.25 grams) kosher salt
¾ teaspoon (1.5 grams) ground nutmeg
¼ teaspoon ground cloves
Whipped Cream (recipe follows)
Garnish: ground cinnamon

1. On a lightly floured surface, roll half of Pie Dough into a 13½-inch circle (³/₁₆ inch thick). Transfer to a 9-inch deep-dish pie plate, pressing into bottom and up sides. Trim edges to ½ inch beyond edge of plate, if needed. Fold edges under, and roll down to edge of plate; crimp, if desired. Reserve any scraps for decorative cutouts. Freeze prepared crust until firm, 20 to 30 minutes.
2. On a lightly floured surface, roll remaining Pie Dough into a 14-inch circle (⅛ inch thick). Using desired small decorative cutters, cut dough, rerolling scraps once. Place cutouts on a parchment paper-lined baking sheet. Refrigerate until firm and ready to use, 20 to 30 minutes.
3. Preheat oven to 375°F (190°C).
4. Lightly dock (prick) prepared crust with a fork. Top with a piece of foil, shiny side up, pressing excess under rim of plate. Add pie weights to fill three-fourths full.
5. Bake until edges start to dry, about 25 minutes. Carefully remove foil and weights, and bake until crust looks dry, about 10 minutes more. (Crust will not have color.) Let cool completely on a wire rack. Leave oven on.
6. In a small bowl, whisk together 1 egg (50 grams) and 1 teaspoon

(5 grams) water. Brush cutouts with egg wash.
7. Bake until lightly golden, about 15 minutes. Reduce oven temperature to 350°F (180°C).
8. In a large bowl, whisk together pumpkin, evaporated milk, sugars, melted butter, vanilla, and remaining 4 eggs (200 grams) until smooth.
9. In a small bowl, whisk together flour, cinnamon, ginger, salt, nutmeg, and cloves. Add flour mixture to pumpkin mixture, and whisk until smooth. Pour into cooled prepared crust, and smooth flat with an offset spatula. Cover edges with foil.
10. Bake for 50 minutes. Carefully remove foil from edges, and cover entire pie with foil. Bake until edges are set but center still jiggles and an instant-read thermometer inserted in center registers 175°F (79°C), 20 to 25 minutes more. Remove foil, and let cool completely on a wire rack, about 2 hours. Decorate the pie with the cutouts as desired. Lightly cover with foil, and refrigerate until ready to serve. Serve room temperature or chilled. Just before serving, top with Whipped Cream, and garnish with cinnamon, if desired.

*We used Bob's Red Mill.

PIE DOUGH
Makes 1 (9-inch) double crust

4 cups (500 grams) all-purpose flour
¼ cup (50 grams) granulated sugar
1 tablespoon (9 grams) kosher salt
1⅓ cups (303 grams) cold unsalted butter, cut into 1-inch cubes
13 to 14 tablespoons (195 to 210 grams) ice water

1. In the work bowl of a food processor, place flour, sugar, and salt; pulse until combined. Add cold butter, and pulse until mixture resembles coarse crumbs and butter is pea-size. With processor running, add 13 tablespoons (195 grams) ice water in a slow, steady stream just until dough comes together; add remaining 1 tablespoon (15 grams) ice water, if needed. (Mixture may appear crumbly. It should be moist and hold together when pinched.) (Alternatively, in a large bowl, stir together flour, sugar, and salt. Using your fingers or a pastry blender, cut in cold butter until mixture resembles coarse crumbs and butter is pea-size. Make a well in center, and add 13 tablespoons (195 grams) ice water; add remaining 1 tablespoon (15 grams) ice water, if needed. Stir with fingers, and knead dough together just until dry ingredients are moistened.)
2. Turn out dough, and lightly knead to bring together. Divide in half (about 530 grams each). Shape each half into a disk. Wrap tightly in plastic wrap, and refrigerate for at least 1 hour. Dough may be refrigerated for up to 3 days or frozen for up to 2 months.

WHIPPED CREAM
Makes 1½ cups

¾ cup (180 grams) cold heavy whipping cream
1½ tablespoons (18 grams) granulated sugar
½ teaspoon (2 grams) vanilla extract

1. In a large bowl, whisk together all ingredients until medium peaks form.

DEEP-DISH CHOCOLATE CHUNK PECAN PIE

Makes 1 (9-inch) deep-dish pie

The only thing that could make golden, rich pecan pie better? Chocolate chunks, stirred into the divinely sweet filling.

Piecrust (recipe follows)
1   cup (336 grams) light corn syrup
¾   cup (150 grams) granulated sugar
⅓   cup (76 grams) unsalted butter, melted
¼   cup (55 grams) firmly packed light brown sugar
4   large eggs (200 grams), lightly beaten
1   tablespoon (13 grams) vanilla extract
¼   teaspoon kosher salt
1½   cups (180 grams) pecan halves
1   cup (180 grams) semisweet chocolate chunks

1. Preheat oven to 350°F (180°C).

2. On a lightly floured surface, roll Piecrust into a 14-inch circle. Transfer to a 9-inch deep-dish pie plate, pressing into bottom and up sides. Trim excess dough to ½ inch beyond edge of pan. Fold edges under, and crimp, if desired.

3. In a large bowl, stir together corn syrup, granulated sugar, melted butter, brown sugar, eggs, vanilla, and salt until well combined. Add pecans and chocolate chunks, stirring until combined. Pour filling into prepared crust.

4. Bake until filling is set and an instant-read thermometer inserted in center registers 200°F (93°C), 1 hour to 1 hour and 10 minutes, covering with foil to prevent excess browning, if necessary. Let cool completely on a wire rack before serving.

PIECRUST

Makes 1 (9-inch) deep-dish crust

2½   cups (313 grams) all-purpose flour
1   teaspoon (3 grams) kosher salt
¾   cup plus 2 tablespoons (198 grams) cold unsalted butter, cubed
7 to 8 tablespoons (105 to 120 grams) ice water

1. In the work bowl of a food processor, place flour and salt; pulse until combined. Add cold butter, and pulse until mixture is crumbly and butter is pea-size. With processor running, add 7 tablespoons (105 grams) ice water in a slow, steady stream just until dough comes together. (Mixture may appear crumbly. It should be moist and hold together when pinched.) Add additional 1 tablespoon (15 grams) ice water only if needed. Turn out dough, and shape into a disk. Wrap tightly in plastic wrap, and refrigerate for at least 1 hour. Dough may be refrigerated for up to 3 days or frozen for up to 2 months. Before using, let Piecrust stand at room temperature until softened, 10 to 15 minutes.

CHOCOLATE HAZELNUT TART

Makes 1 (9-inch) tart

A delectable complement to your favorite red wine, this creamy tart is all things sweet and salty with cranberry filling and a hazelnut garnish.

Chocolate Short Dough (recipe follows)
1 cup (200 grams) granulated sugar
⅔ cup (226 grams) dark corn syrup
¼ cup (57 grams) unsalted butter, melted
¼ cup (60 grams) dry red wine
2 large eggs (100 grams)
2 teaspoons (8 grams) vanilla extract
1½ cups (255 grams) fresh or frozen cranberries
1 cup (144 grams) peeled hazelnuts, skins removed and roughly chopped
1 cup (170 grams) semisweet chocolate chips
½ cup (120 grams) heavy whipping cream
Garnish: chopped hazelnuts, flaked sea salt

1. Preheat oven to 350°F (180°C).
2. On a lightly floured surface, roll Chocolate Short Dough into a 12-inch circle. Transfer to a 9-inch fluted square removable-bottom tart pan, pressing into bottom and up sides. Top with a piece of parchment paper, letting ends extend over edges of pan. Add pie weights.
3. Bake for 15 minutes. Carefully remove parchment and weights. Bake for 5 minutes more. Let cool completely on a wire rack.
4. In a medium saucepan, stir together sugar, corn syrup, melted butter, wine, eggs, and vanilla until smooth. Stir in cranberries and hazelnuts. Bring to a boil over medium-high heat, stirring frequently. Reduce heat to medium-low; simmer, stirring constantly, until thickened, 6 to 8 minutes. Let cool to room temperature.
5. Spoon cranberry filling into cooled prepared crust, smoothing top with an offset spatula.
6. In a medium heatproof bowl, place chocolate chips.
7. In a small saucepan, heat cream over medium-high heat just until bubbles form around edges of pan. (Do not boil.) Pour warm cream over chocolate; cover and let stand for 5 minutes. Whisk until smooth. Pour ganache over cranberry filling, smoothing to edges. Refrigerate until chilled, at least 3 hours.
8. Remove from pan. Garnish with hazelnuts and sea salt, if desired.

CHOCOLATE SHORT DOUGH
Makes 1 (9-inch) crust

9 tablespoons (126 grams) unsalted butter, softened
⅓ cup (67 grams) granulated sugar
2 large egg yolks (37 grams)
1½ cups (188 grams) all-purpose flour
¼ cup (21 grams) unsweetened cocoa powder
¼ teaspoon kosher salt

1. In a large bowl, beat butter and sugar with a mixer at medium speed until fluffy, 3 to 4 minutes, stopping to scrape sides of bowl. Add egg yolks, one at a time, beating well after each addition.
2. In a medium bowl, sift together flour and cocoa. Add flour mixture and salt to butter mixture, and beat at low speed just until combined. (Do not overmix.)
3. Shape dough into a disk; wrap dough in plastic wrap, and refrigerate until chilled, at least 1 hour, before using.

PEACH PIE

Makes 1 (9-inch) pie

Fresh peaches, buttery piecrust, and a straight-up bonkers streusel make this pie an absolute favorite. Don't be surprised if serving a single slice elicits wild proclamations of undying love.

3   pounds (1,361 grams) fresh peaches, peeled, pitted, and sliced
1   cup (200 grams) plus 2 tablespoons (24 grams) granulated sugar, divided
1   lemon (99 grams), zested and juiced
½   teaspoon (1.5 grams) kosher salt
½   recipe Our Favorite Piecrust (recipe on page 61)
1   tablespoon (8 grams) cornstarch
2   tablespoons (18 grams) low-sugar fruit pectin
1   vanilla bean, split lengthwise, seeds scraped and reserved
1   teaspoon grated fresh nutmeg
Browned Butter Pecan Streusel (recipe follows)

1. In a large bowl, toss together peaches, 1 cup (200 grams) sugar, lemon zest and juice, and salt. Let stand for 30 minutes.
2. Let Our Favorite Piecrust stand at room temperature until slightly softened, about 5 minutes. On a lightly floured surface, roll dough into a 12-inch circle. Transfer to a 9-inch pie plate, pressing into bottom and up sides. Trim excess dough to ½ inch beyond edge of plate. Fold edges under. Reroll scraps; using a decorative cutter, cut dough. Place on outer edge of crust. Freeze for 30 minutes.
3. Transfer 1 cup (188 grams) peach mixture to a small bowl, and mash with a fork. Strain remaining peach mixture through a colander, reserving ½ cup (120 grams) peach liquid. Return drained peaches to large bowl, and toss with cornstarch.
4. Preheat oven to 400°F (200°C).
5. In a small skillet, whisk together reserved ½ cup (120 grams) peach liquid, pectin, reserved vanilla bean seeds, nutmeg, and remaining 2 tablespoons (24 grams) sugar. Cook over medium heat until pectin is dissolved and mixture thickens slightly, 3 to 4 minutes.
6. Toss together drained peaches and mashed peaches; pour into prepared crust. Drizzle with pectin mixture. Top with Browned Butter Pecan Streusel. Place on a baking sheet.
7. Bake for 20 minutes. Reduce oven temperature to 375°F (190°C), and cover loosely with foil. Bake until golden brown and bubbly, 30 to 35 minutes more.

BROWNED BUTTER PECAN STREUSEL
Makes about 1½ cups

¼   cup (57 grams) unsalted butter
½   cup plus 1 tablespoon (71 grams) all-purpose flour
⅓   cup (38 grams) chopped toasted pecans
¼   cup (50 grams) granulated sugar
2   tablespoons (28 grams) firmly packed dark brown sugar
1   teaspoon (3 grams) kosher salt

1. In a small light-colored saucepan, melt butter over medium heat. Cook until butter solids turns a medium-brown color and butter has a nutty aroma, about 10 minutes. Remove from heat, and let cool slightly.
2. In a medium bowl, whisk together flour, pecans, sugars, and salt. Drizzle with browned butter, and stir with a wooden spoon until combined. Crumble with fingertips until desired consistency is reached.

PINEAPPLE AND COCONUT PIE

Makes 1 (9-inch) pie

Think of this tropical dish as a piña colada in pie form, minus the paper umbrella and rum.

3   cups (375 grams) all-purpose flour
1   tablespoon (12 grams) granulated sugar
2   teaspoons (6 grams) kosher salt
1   cup (227 grams) cold unsalted butter, cubed
⅓   cup plus 2 teaspoons (90 grams) ice water
2   tablespoons (6 grams) orange zest
2   tablespoons (30 grams) fresh orange juice
1   large egg (50 grams)
1   teaspoon (5 grams) water
4   cups (800 grams) ¼-inch-sliced cored peeled fresh pineapple
Toasted Coconut Pastry Cream (recipe follows)
Garnish: toasted flaked coconut

1. In the work bowl of a food processor, place flour, sugar, and salt; pulse until combined. Add cold butter, pulsing until mixture is crumbly. Add ⅓ cup plus 2 teaspoons (90 grams) ice water and orange zest and juice, pulsing until dough just comes together. Divide dough in half, and shape each half into a disk. Wrap tightly in plastic wrap, and refrigerate for 30 minutes.
2. Preheat oven to 350°F (180°C).
3. On a lightly floured surface, roll half of dough into a 12-inch circle. Transfer to a 9-inch pie plate, pressing into bottom and up sides. Trim excess dough to ½ inch beyond edge of plate. Fold edges under. Prick bottom and sides of dough with a fork. Refrigerate for at least 30 minutes.
4. On a lightly floured surface, roll remaining dough into a 10-inch circle. Using a sharp knife, cut ¼-inch-wide strips. Braid dough strips, pinching ends to seal.
5. Brush water on rim of prepared dough in plate. Place braided

dough along brushed rim. Overlap end pieces, and pinch together to seal. In a small bowl, whisk together egg and 1 teaspoon (5 grams) water; lightly brush over dough.
6. Top dough with a piece of parchment paper, letting ends extend over edges of plate. Add pie weights.
7. Bake for 15 minutes. Carefully remove paper and weights. Bake until golden brown, about 15 minutes more. Let cool for 10 minutes.
8. Arrange 1 cup (200 grams) pineapple in bottom of prepared crust. Top with Toasted Coconut Pastry Cream. Top with remaining 3 cups (600 grams) pineapple. Garnish with coconut, if desired.

TOASTED COCONUT PASTRY CREAM
Makes about 2 cups

1   cup (240 grams) whole milk
1   cup (240 grams) unsweetened coconut milk
⅔   cup (133 grams) granulated sugar, divided
4½   tablespoons (36 grams) cornstarch
5   large egg yolks (93 grams)
2   tablespoons (28 grams) unsalted butter, softened
⅔   cup (56 grams) unsweetened flaked coconut, toasted

1. In a medium saucepan, bring milk, coconut milk, and ⅓ cup (66.5 grams) sugar to a boil over medium heat.
2. In a medium bowl, whisk together cornstarch, egg yolks, and remaining ⅓ cup (66.5 grams) sugar until combined. Whisking constantly, add 1 cup (240 grams) hot milk mixture to yolk mixture. Pour warm yolk mixture into remaining hot milk mixture in saucepan. Cook, whisking constantly, until thickened, 1 to 2 minutes. Remove from heat, and add butter. Fold in coconut.
3. Pour mixture onto a rimmed half-sheet pan, and cover with a piece of plastic wrap, pressing wrap directly onto surface. Let cool to room temperature before using.

BLUEBERRY PIE

Makes 1 (9-inch) pie

This pie is made with the freshest blueberries—and not much else! We'd happily eat this one morning, noon, and night.

Our Favorite Piecrust (recipe on page 61)
1   pound (454 grams) fresh blueberries
1   cup (200 grams) granulated sugar
1   lemon (99 grams), zested and juiced
1   vanilla bean, split lengthwise, seeds scraped and reserved
3   tablespoons (24 grams) cornstarch
1   teaspoon (3 grams) kosher salt
1   large egg (50 grams), lightly beaten
2   tablespoons (24 grams) turbinado sugar

1. Let Our Favorite Piecrust stand at room temperature until slightly softened, about 5 minutes. On a lightly floured surface, roll half of dough into a 12-inch circle. Transfer to a 9-inch pie plate, pressing into bottom and up sides. Trim excess dough to ½ inch beyond edge of plate. Fold edges under. Freeze for 30 minutes.
2. Preheat oven to 375°F (190°C).
3. In a medium saucepan, combine blueberries, granulated sugar, lemon zest and juice, reserved vanilla bean seeds, cornstarch, and salt over medium heat. Stir gently, being careful not to crush berries. Bring to a gentle boil, and cook until thickened, stirring constantly, 5 to 10 minutes. Remove from heat, and let cool. Pour filling into prepared crust.

4. On a lightly floured surface, roll remaining dough to ¼-inch thickness. Using a sharp knife, cut dough into ½-inch-wide strips. Braid dough strips, and arrange on top of filling, tucking ends under. Reroll scraps, and cut remaining dough into long ¼-inch-wide strips. Braid dough strips, and arrange around edge of crust. Brush dough with egg, and sprinkle with turbinado sugar. Place on a baking sheet.
5. Bake until golden brown and bubbly, 40 to 50 minutes, covering with foil halfway through baking to prevent excess browning, if necessary. Let cool completely before serving.

PLUM PIE

Makes 1 (9-inch) pie

Sweet and spicy, this plum pie makes the most of summer's stone fruit bounty. Ginger and black pepper add a subtle kick. Serve with ice cream for an extra-special treat.

2	pounds (907 grams) plums (8 to 10 plums), pitted and sliced
1	cup (200 grams) plus 1 tablespoon (12 grams) granulated sugar, divided
1	lemon (99 grams), zested and juiced
2	teaspoons grated fresh ginger
1	teaspoon (3 grams) kosher salt
1	teaspoon (2 grams) ground ginger
½	teaspoon (1 gram) ground black pepper

Our Favorite Piecrust (recipe on page 61)

2	tablespoons (18 grams) low-sugar fruit pectin
3	tablespoons (24 grams) cornstarch
1	large egg (50 grams), lightly beaten
2	tablespoons (24 grams) turbinado sugar

1. In a large bowl, toss together plums, 1 cup (200 grams) granulated sugar, lemon zest and juice, fresh ginger, salt, ground ginger, and pepper. Let stand for 30 minutes.

2. Let Our Favorite Piecrust stand at room temperature until slightly softened, about 5 minutes. On a lightly floured surface, roll half of dough into a 12-inch circle. Transfer to a 9-inch pie plate, pressing into bottom and up sides. Trim excess dough to ½ inch beyond edge of plate. Fold edges under, and crimp, if desired. Freeze for 30 minutes.

3. Preheat oven to 400°F (200°C).

4. Strain plum mixture through a colander, reserving ½ cup (120 grams) plum liquid.

5. In a small saucepan, combine reserved ½ cup (120 grams) plum liquid, pectin, and remaining 1 tablespoon (12 grams) granulated sugar. Cook over medium-high heat, whisking constantly, until pectin is dissolved and mixture thickens slightly, 3 to 4 minutes.

6. Toss together plum mixture and cornstarch; pour into prepared crust. Drizzle with pectin mixture.

7. On a lightly floured surface, roll remaining dough into a 12-inch circle. Cut dough into triangles, and layer on top of filling. Brush dough with egg, and sprinkle with turbinado sugar. Place on a baking sheet.

8. Bake for 20 minutes. Reduce oven temperature to 375°F (190°C), and bake until golden brown and bubbly, 35 to 40 minutes more, covering with foil to prevent excess browning, if necessary. Let cool for at least 1 hour before serving.

KEY LIME PIE

Makes 1 (9-inch) pie

Our take on the beloved original features a salty-sweet crust and intense lime flavor thanks to a cup of juice from this pie's tiny namesake citrus.

1¼ cups (150 grams) graham cracker crumbs
¼ cup (55 grams) firmly packed light brown sugar
¼ cup (57 grams) unsalted butter, melted
½ teaspoon (1.5 grams) kosher salt
2 (14-ounce) cans (760 grams) sweetened condensed milk
1 cup (240 grams) Key lime juice (from bottle)*
2 large eggs (100 grams)
1½ cups (360 grams) heavy whipping cream
¼ cup (30 grams) confectioners' sugar

1. Preheat oven to 350°F (180°C).
2. In a medium bowl, stir together graham cracker crumbs, brown sugar, melted butter, and salt. Using a measuring cup, press mixture into bottom and up sides of a 9-inch pie plate.
3. Bake until lightly browned, about 10 minutes. Let cool completely.
4. In a large bowl, whisk together condensed milk, lime juice, and eggs until combined. Pour into prepared crust.
5. Bake until set, about 10 minutes. Let cool completely.
6. In the bowl of a stand mixer fitted with the whisk attachment, beat cream and confectioners' sugar at high speed until stiff peaks form, 2 to 3 minutes. Spread whipped cream over pie.

Regular lime juice may be substituted.

AROUND
THE WORLD
IN PIES

SHOWCASING RECIPES THAT SPAN THE GLOBE, THIS EXPLORATION
OF PIES AND TARTS WILL TAKE YOU ON THE ULTIMATE CULINARY
ADVENTURE—FROM AN AUSTRIAN LINZER TORTE TO THE SWEET
EGG TARTS FAVORED IN HONG KONG

SUGAR PIE

Makes 1 (9-inch) pie

Recipe by Emily Turner

For Quebecers, sugar pie, or tarte au sucre, *is synonymous with Christmas indulgence. Brought to Quebec by French immigrants, this sweet pie combines brown sugar and maple syrup, a combo that slowly caramelizes while baking, creating a light crunchy top and a custard-like silky interior.*

Butter Piecrust (recipe follows)
1½ cups (330 grams) firmly packed light brown sugar
¼ cup (85 grams) maple syrup
3 tablespoons (24 grams) all-purpose flour
2 large egg yolks (37 grams)
1 large egg (50 grams)
1 cup (240 grams) heavy whipping cream
3 tablespoons (42 grams) unsalted butter
1 teaspoon (4 grams) vanilla extract
¼ teaspoon kosher salt
Garnish: confectioners' sugar

1. On a lightly floured surface, roll Butter Piecrust to ¼-inch thickness. Transfer to a 9-inch pie plate, pressing into bottom and up sides. Trim excess dough. Fold edges under, and crimp, if desired. Freeze for 10 minutes.
2. Preheat oven to 400°F (200°C).
3. Top dough with a piece of parchment paper, letting ends extend over edges of plate. Add pie weights.
4. Bake until edges are set, about 10 minutes. Carefully remove parchment and weights. Bake until bottom of crust is set, about 2 minutes more. Reduce oven temperature to 350°F (180°C).
5. In a large bowl, whisk together brown sugar, maple syrup, flour, egg yolks, and egg until smooth.
6. In a small saucepan, bring cream and butter to a simmer over medium-high heat. Whisking constantly, slowly pour hot cream mixture into sugar mixture. Whisk in vanilla and salt. Strain mixture through a fine-mesh sieve, discarding solids. Pour filling into prepared crust. Loosely cover with foil.
7. Bake in bottom third of oven until crust is golden brown and filling is set (center should still jiggle slightly), 50 to 55 minutes. Let cool completely. Garnish with confectioners' sugar, if desired.

Butter Piecrust
Makes 1 (9-inch) crust

2½ cups (313 grams) all-purpose flour
2 tablespoons (24 grams) granulated sugar
1½ teaspoons (4.5 grams) kosher salt
¾ cup (170 grams) cold unsalted butter, cubed
½ cup (120 grams) ice water

1. In the work bowl of a food processor, place flour, sugar, and salt; pulse until combined. Add cold butter, and pulse until mixture is crumbly. Add ½ cup (120 grams) ice water, 2 tablespoons (30 grams) at a time, just until dough comes together (you may not need all of the water). Shape dough into a disk, and wrap tightly in plastic wrap. Refrigerate until chilled, about 2 hours.

Photo by Maya Visnyei

CHERRY-HAZELNUT SHEKERBURA

Makes 14 shekerbura

Shekerbura *is a traditional sweet pastry hailing from Azerbaijan, a country located at the crossroads of Southwest Asia and southeastern Europe. We added cherry and hazelnut liqueur to the dessert's standard filling of ground nuts and sugar. Yeasted dough lets the pastry's surface serve as a palette for intricate, textured patterns. We love how the thin, elevated ridges turn a deep golden brown while baking for even more visual contrast.*

2⅔ cups (334 grams) all-purpose flour
⅔ cup (150 grams) unsalted butter, softened
½ cup (48 grams) hazelnut meal
¼ teaspoon ground cinnamon
¼ teaspoon ground black pepper
½ cup (120 grams) sour cream
2 large egg yolks (37 grams)
1½ teaspoons (4.5 grams) kosher salt
2 tablespoons (30 grams) warm whole milk (105°F/40°C to 110°F/43°C)
1 tablespoon (12 grams) granulated sugar
½ teaspoon (1 gram) instant yeast
1 large egg (50 grams)
1 teaspoon (5 grams) water
Cherry-Hazelnut Filling (recipe follows)

1. In a large bowl, combine flour, butter, hazelnut meal, cinnamon, and pepper. Rub with fingertips until well combined. Set aside.
2. In a small bowl, stir together sour cream, egg yolks, and salt. In another small bowl, combine warm milk, sugar, and yeast. Let stand until slightly bubbly, about 2 minutes.
3. Add sour cream mixture and yeast mixture to flour mixture; stir until combined. Turn out dough onto a lightly floured surface, and knead until smooth, about 2 minutes. Return to bowl; cover with plastic wrap, and let rest for 30 minutes.
4. Preheat oven to 350°F (180°C). Line 2 baking sheets with parchment paper.
5. In a small bowl, whisk together egg and 1 teaspoon (5 grams) water. Divide dough into 14 equal pieces. Working with one piece at a time, shape each piece into a 4½-inch round. Brush edges with egg wash. Spoon Cherry-Hazelnut Filling into center of each round, dividing evenly among rounds. Fold dough over filling, and crimp edges as desired. Place on prepared pans.

6. Using a straight fondant crimper, pinch a row of lines ¼ inch apart into top of crust at a 45-degree angle. Repeat rows 2 more times, rotating direction of lines by 180 degrees each time. Using a paring knife, cut 2 small vents in top of each shekerbura, and brush lightly with egg wash.
7. Bake until crust is lightly golden and fruit is bubbly, 20 to 25 minutes. Let cool completely. Store in an airtight container for up to 1 day.

> **PRO TIP**
> A *maggash*, pastry tongs with serrated tips, is traditionally used to create the designs in the dough before baking. We used a fondant crimper, which can be found at most craft stores or large online retailers.

CHERRY-HAZELNUT FILLING
Makes about 1¾ cups

⅔ pound (302 grams) fresh cherries, pitted
⅔ cup (147 grams) firmly packed light brown sugar
½ cup (64 grams) dried cherries
2 tablespoons (16 grams) cornstarch
1 tablespoon (3 grams) lemon zest
1 tablespoon (15 grams) fresh lemon juice
1 tablespoon (15 grams) hazelnut liqueur*
½ teaspoon (1.5 grams) kosher salt
¼ teaspoon ground black pepper
¼ teaspoon ground cinnamon

1. In a medium saucepan, combine all ingredients. Cook over medium-low heat until cherries have released their juices, about 2 minutes. Increase heat to medium, and cook, stirring occasionally, until juices have thickened, 5 to 7 minutes. Remove from heat, and let cool completely. Refrigerate in an airtight container for up to 3 days.

We used Frangelico.

BLUEBERRY BRETON TARTS

Makes 20 mini tarts

For this ode to blueberries, we paired slivers of dried pears with a dried blueberry, lemon, and gin-flavored filling.

4   large egg yolks (74 grams)
¾   cup (150 grams) granulated sugar
¾   cup (170 grams) unsalted butter, softened and cubed
¾   teaspoon (2.25 grams) kosher salt
1¾   cups (219 grams) all-purpose flour
¾   cup (94 grams) cake flour
⅓   cup (43 grams) diced dried pear
1½   tablespoons (22.5 grams) baking powder
¾   teaspoon (1.5 grams) ground juniper berries
½   teaspoon (1 gram) ground black pepper
Lemon Blueberry Filling (recipe follows)
Toasty Brown Sugar Pastry Cream (recipe follows)

1. In the bowl of a stand mixer fitted with the paddle attachment, beat egg yolks and sugar at medium speed until pale yellow, 2 to 3 minutes. Add butter and salt, beating until combined.

2. In a medium bowl, whisk together flours, pear, baking powder, juniper berries, and pepper. With mixer on low speed, gradually add flour mixture to yolk mixture, beating just until combined. Turn out dough, and divide in half. Shape each half into a disk. Wrap in plastic wrap, and refrigerate for at least 30 minutes.

3. Preheat oven to 325°F (170°C). Line a baking sheet with parchment paper. Place 5 (2½-inch) round cutters on pan; butter and flour parchment and cutters.

4. On a lightly floured surface, roll half of dough to ¼-inch thickness. Using a 2½-inch round cutter, cut 5 rounds from dough. Place rounds in prepared cutters. Reserve dough scraps, and keep refrigerated. Using a rounded teaspoon, press a slight indentation into center of each round.

5. Bake until puffed and golden brown, about 15 minutes. Let cool completely. Carefully remove cutters, transfer pastry to wire racks, and let cool completely. Repeat procedure with remaining dough, buttering and flouring cutters each time. Spoon 1½ teaspoons Lemon Blueberry Filling into each Breton crust. Pipe Toasty Brown Sugar Pastry Cream around edges of tarts in desired pattern. Serve immediately.

LEMON BLUEBERRY FILLING

Makes ½ cup

⅓   cup (43 grams) dried blueberries
¼   cup (80 grams) blueberry preserves
¼   cup (55 grams) firmly packed light brown sugar
2   teaspoons (10 grams) unsalted butter
2   teaspoons (4 grams) lemon zest
1   teaspoon (5 grams) gin

1. In a small saucepan, bring dried blueberries and water to cover by 1 inch to a boil over high heat. Reduce heat to low; cook until blueberries are softened, about 15 minutes. Drain blueberries, reserving 2 teaspoons (10 grams) cooking liquid.

2. In the work bowl of a food processor, place warm blueberries, reserved 2 teaspoons (10 grams) cooking liquid, blueberry preserves, brown sugar, butter, zest, and gin; pulse until mixture has the texture of jam. Let cool completely. Refrigerate in an airtight container for up to 1 week.

TOASTY BROWN SUGAR PASTRY CREAM

Makes about 2¾ cups

1½   cups (360 grams) heavy whipping cream
¾   cup (180 grams) whole milk
1   large egg (50 grams)
2   large egg yolks (37 grams)
⅓   cup (73 grams) firmly packed light brown sugar
4½   tablespoons (36 grams) cornstarch
1½   tablespoons (21 grams) toasted sesame oil

1. In a medium saucepan, heat cream and milk over medium heat until steaming.

2. In a medium bowl, whisk together egg, egg yolks, brown sugar, and cornstarch. Whisking constantly, slowly add hot cream mixture to egg mixture. Return cream mixture to saucepan, and cook, whisking constantly, until thickened.

3. Transfer to a medium bowl, and stir in oil. Press a piece of plastic wrap directly onto surface of pastry cream to prevent a skin from forming. Refrigerate for 1 hour.

ASSAM TREACLE TART

Makes 1 (9-inch) tart

A standard of British baking, treacle tart is known for its simple but delicious bread crumb, golden syrup, and lemon-scented filling. In this aromatic twist on Harry Potter's favorite dessert, Assam-infused pastry balances the classic, gooey treacle filling.

Assam Tart Dough (recipe follows)
1   large egg (50 grams)
1   tablespoon (15 grams) heavy whipping cream
1¾ cups (591 grams) golden syrup
4¼ cups (155 grams) fresh white bread crumbs
¼   cup (12 grams) lemon zest
¼   cup (60 grams) fresh lemon juice

1. Preheat oven to 375°F (190°C). Butter and flour a 9-inch fluted round removable-bottom tart pan. Line a large plate with parchment paper.
2. On a lightly floured surface, roll two-thirds of Assam Tart Dough into a 12-inch circle. Transfer to prepared pan, pressing into bottom and up sides. Roll remaining dough to ⅛-inch thickness. Using a sharp knife, cut dough into 1x¼-inch rectangles. Place on prepared plate.
3. In a small bowl, whisk together egg and cream. Brush egg wash onto crust. Prick crust with a fork 6 times.
4. In a medium saucepan, heat golden syrup over medium-low heat until melted. (Do not boil.) Add bread crumbs and lemon zest and juice, stirring until combined. Pour filling into prepared crust. Top with rectangles in desired pattern. Brush egg wash onto rectangles.
5. Bake until crust is golden brown and filling is set, 30 to 35 minutes, covering with foil halfway through baking to prevent excess browning, if necessary. Serve warm or cold. Cover and refrigerate for up to 4 days.

Assam Tart Dough
Makes 1 (9-inch) crust and lattice

3   cups (375 grams) all-purpose flour
1   tablespoon (6 grams) Assam loose tea
¾   teaspoon (2.25 grams) kosher salt
¾   cup (170 grams) cold unsalted butter, cubed
⅓   cup (80 grams) ice water

1. In the work bowl of a food processor, place flour, loose tea, and salt; pulse until combined. Add cold butter, and pulse until mixture is crumbly. With processor running, add ⅓ cup (80 grams) ice water in a slow, steady stream until dough comes together. Wrap in plastic wrap, and refrigerate for at least 30 minutes.

MAIDS OF HONOR TARTS

Makes 12 tartlets

Recipe by Lisa Heathcote

Made with jam and a lightly spiced cottage cheese filling, these tarts were a go-to recipe of renowned food stylist Lisa Heathcote for Downton Abbey, *the hit PBS television series and feature film. Maids of honour tarts are said to go back to the time of King Henry VIII of England. Supposedly, when Henry noticed Anne Boleyn, then still a maid, savoring these tarts with other ladies in waiting, he decided to try some for himself. He found them so delicious that he named them after the maids.*

Puff Pastry Dough (recipe follows)
3½ tablespoons (50 grams) unsalted butter, softened
¼   cup (50 grams) castor sugar
½   cup (50 grams) almond flour
1   medium free-range egg (47 grams), beaten
6   tablespoons (18 grams) lemon zest
1   tablespoon (8 grams) all-purpose flour
½   teaspoon grated fresh nutmeg or ground mace
14 tablespoons (100 grams) full-fat small-curd cottage cheese
6   teaspoons (42 grams) raspberry jam

1. Preheat oven to 350°F (180°C).
2. Roll Puff Pastry Dough to ¹⁄₁₆-inch thickness. Using a 3½-inch round cutter, cut 12 rounds. Transfer to a 12-cup muffin pan, pressing into bottom and up sides of each cup. Refrigerate while preparing filling.
3. In a large bowl, stir together butter and castor sugar with a wooden spoon until creamy and mixture turns pale, 2 to 3 minutes. Add almond flour, egg, lemon zest, all-purpose flour, and nutmeg or mace, stirring until combined. Stir in cottage cheese.
4. Spoon ½ teaspoon (3.5 grams) jam into each prepared crust. Divide cottage cheese mixture among prepared crusts.
5. Bake until risen and lightly browned on top, about 25 minutes. Let cool completely on a wire rack.

PUFF PASTRY DOUGH

Makes enough dough for 12 tartlets

½   cup (113 grams) unsalted butter, cubed
1   cup (125 grams) all-purpose flour
1   teaspoon (3 grams) kosher salt
3½ tablespoons (52 grams) ice water

1. Freeze butter for 30 minutes.
2. In the work bowl of a food processor, place flour and salt; pulse until combined. Add frozen butter, and pulse until butter is dime-size. With processor running, gradually add 3½ tablespoons (52 grams) ice water just until mixture forms a ball.
3. Turn out dough onto a lightly floured surface, and shape into a disk. Wrap in plastic wrap, and refrigerate for at least 30 minutes.

AUTHENTIC IRISH APPLE TARTS

Makes 6 (4- to 4½-inch) tarts

Recipe by Allie Roomberg

This recipe embodies the Irish classic in every way, from the buttery crust to the nutty filling to the crumbly streusel topping. And, of course, tender apples play the starring role!

Tart Dough (recipe follows)
1½ cups (144 grams) almond meal
⅔ cup (133 grams) granulated sugar
¼ cup (60 grams) apple brandy
2 large eggs (100 grams)
2 tablespoons (28 grams) unsalted butter, melted
1 tablespoon (3 grams) lemon zest (about 1 lemon)
1 teaspoon (4 grams) vanilla extract
¼ teaspoon kosher salt
4 medium Granny Smith apples (560 grams)
2 tablespoons (40 grams) warm apple jelly
Crumb Topping (recipe follows)
Custard Sauce (recipe follows)
Vanilla ice cream, to serve
Garnish: confectioners' sugar

1. Preheat oven to 375°F (190°C).
2. Turn out Tart Dough onto a lightly floured surface, and divide into 6 portions (about 62 grams each). Roll each portion into a 7-inch circle, and transfer each to a 4- to 4½-inch fluted round removable-bottom tart pan, lightly pressing into bottom and up sides. Trim off excess. Using a fork, prick bottoms a few times.
3. Bake for 10 minutes. (If crust puffs up in middle, press down gently while still warm.) Leave oven on.
4. In a large bowl, stir together almond meal, granulated sugar, brandy, eggs, melted butter, lemon zest, vanilla extract, and salt. Divide among prepared crusts.
5. Peel apples, and cut in half; core each half, and cut into ⅛-inch-thick slices, making sure to keep slices grouped together. Fan apple slices on top of filling. Brush apples with jelly, and top with Crumb Topping.
6. Bake until crust is just golden around edges and apples are tender, 20 to 25 minutes for 4-inch tarts or about 35 minutes for 4½-inch tarts. Remove from pans. Serve warm with Custard Sauce and ice cream. Garnish with confectioners' sugar, if desired. Refrigerate in an airtight container for up to 5 days.

TART DOUGH
Makes 6 (4- to 4½-inch) crusts

1½ cups (188 grams) all-purpose flour
⅓ cup (40 grams) confectioners' sugar
¼ teaspoon kosher salt
½ cup (113 grams) cold unsalted butter, cubed
1 large egg yolk (19 grams)
1½ tablespoons (22.5 grams) heavy whipping cream
½ teaspoon (2 grams) vanilla extract

1. In the work bowl of a food processor, place flour, confectioners' sugar, and salt; pulse until combined. Add cold butter, and pulse until mixture resembles coarse bread crumbs. Add egg yolk, cream, and vanilla, and process until dough forms a ball and pulls away cleanly from sides of bowl.

Note: *It is not necessary to chill this dough.*

CRUMB TOPPING
Makes about 1½ cups

6 tablespoons (84 grams) unsalted butter
1½ cups (188 grams) all-purpose flour
½ cup (100 grams) granulated sugar
1 tablespoon (3 grams) lemon zest (about 1 lemon)
¼ teaspoon kosher salt

1. In a small saucepan, melt butter over medium-low heat. Remove from heat; using a fork, stir in flour, sugar, lemon zest, and salt until combined and mixture is crumbly. Let cool completely before using.

Note: *Crumb Topping can be made a few days ahead; refrigerate in an airtight container until ready to use. Extra topping can be stored in the freezer for other uses.*

CUSTARD SAUCE
Makes about 2 cups

1 cup (240 grams) whole milk
¾ cup (180 grams) heavy whipping cream
1 medium vanilla bean, split lengthwise, seeds scraped and reserved
4 large egg yolks (74 grams)
⅓ cup (67 grams) granulated sugar

1. In a small saucepan, combine milk, cream, and vanilla bean and reserved seeds. Heat over medium-low heat just until bubbles form around edges of pan. (Do not boil.) Discard vanilla bean.
2. In a medium bowl, whisk together egg yolks and sugar. Gradually

add warm milk mixture to egg yolk mixture, whisking constantly. Return mixture to saucepan, and cook over low heat, whisking constantly, until slightly thickened and mixture can coat the back of a wooden spoon, about 5 minutes. (Mixture will continue to thicken as it cools.) Strain through a fine-mesh sieve into a heatproof bowl. Place bowl in an ice water bath until sauce is chilled. Remove bowl from ice water bath, cover sauce with plastic wrap, and refrigerate until ready to use.

Note: *Custard Sauce can be made 1 day ahead; refrigerate in an airtight container until ready to use.*

Photo by Allie Roomberg

BAKEWELL TART

Makes 1 (9-inch) tart

Fans of frangipane, rejoice: this Bakewell Tart is the dessert for you. Instead of the traditional raspberry jam this legendary British recipe calls for, we used sweet plum preserves. Amp up the almond even further with our glaze flavored with almond liqueur.

Pâte Sablée (recipe follows)
¾ cup (240 grams) plum preserves*
½ cup (113 grams) unsalted butter, softened
½ cup (100 grams) granulated sugar
2 large eggs (100 grams)
1 tablespoon (15 grams) almond liqueur
1¼ cups (120 grams) almond flour
2 tablespoons (16 grams) all-purpose flour
⅓ cup (38 grams) sliced almonds
Almond Glaze (recipe follows)

1. Preheat oven to 325°F (170°C).
2. On a lightly floured surface, roll Pâte Sablée into an 11-inch circle, about ¼ inch thick. Transfer to a 9-inch fluted round removable-bottom tart pan, gently pressing into bottom and up sides. Trim excess dough. Freeze until hard, about 10 minutes. Prick bottom of dough with a fork. Top with a piece of parchment paper, letting ends extend over edges of pan. Add pie weights.
3. Bake until edges look dry, about 15 minutes. Carefully remove parchment and weights. Bake until crust is dry, about 10 minutes more. Let cool completely on a wire rack.
4. Preheat oven to 350°F (180°C).
5. Spread preserves into prepared Pâte Sablée. Refrigerate while preparing filling.
6. In the bowl of a stand mixer fitted with the paddle attachment, beat butter and sugar at medium speed until creamy, 3 to 4 minutes, stopping to scrape sides of bowl. Add eggs, one at a time, beating well after each addition. Beat in liqueur.
7. In a medium bowl, whisk together flours. With mixer on low speed, gradually add flour mixture to butter mixture, beating just until combined. Spread filling onto preserves, and sprinkle with almonds.
8. Bake until golden and set, 45 to 50 minutes. Let cool in pan for 15 minutes. Remove from pan, and drizzle with Almond Glaze. Serve warm or at room temperature.

We used Wilkin & Sons Tiptree Damson Preserves.

PÂTE SABLÉE
Makes dough for 1 (9-inch) crust

½ cup (113 grams) unsalted butter, softened
⅓ cup (40 grams) confectioners' sugar
1 tablespoon (3 grams) lemon zest
½ teaspoon (1.5 grams) kosher salt
1 large egg yolk (19 grams)
1½ cups (188 grams) pastry flour

1. In the bowl of a stand mixer fitted with the paddle attachment, beat butter at medium speed until smooth, about 1 minute. Add confectioners' sugar, lemon zest, and salt, and beat until smooth, about 1 minute. Add egg yolk, and beat until combined, about 1 minute. Add flour in two additions, beating just until combined after each addition. Turn out dough onto a lightly floured surface, and gently knead 3 to 4 times. Shape dough into a disk, and wrap in plastic wrap. Refrigerate for 1 hour.

ALMOND GLAZE
Makes ¼ cup

½ cup (60 grams) confectioners' sugar
4 teaspoons (20 grams) almond liqueur

1. In a medium bowl, whisk together confectioners' sugar and liqueur until smooth. Use immediately.

SWEET EGG TARTS

Makes 8 (2½-inch) tarts

We kept our egg tarts simple and classic to the Hong Kong formula, with a tender pâte sucrée crust holding a glistening custard filling.

⅓   cup (76 grams) unsalted butter, softened
¼   cup (30 grams) confectioners' sugar
½   teaspoon kosher salt, divided
4   large egg yolks (75 grams), room temperature and divided
¾   teaspoon (3 grams) vanilla extract, divided
1   cup (125 grams) all-purpose flour
¼   cup (31 grams) unbleached cake flour
¼   cup (60 grams) water
2½   tablespoons (30 grams) granulated sugar
2½   tablespoons (37.5 grams) evaporated milk

1. In the bowl of a stand mixer fitted with the paddle attachment, beat butter, confectioners' sugar, and ¼ teaspoon salt at medium speed until creamy, 1 to 2 minutes, stopping to scrape sides of bowl. Add 1 egg yolk (19 grams); beat until well combined. Beat in ¼ teaspoon (1 gram) vanilla.

2. In a medium bowl, whisk together flours. With mixer on low speed, gradually add flour mixture to butter mixture, beating just until a dough forms.

3. Spray 8 (2½-inch) fluted round tart pans with baking spray with flour; place on a rimmed baking sheet.

4. Divide dough into 8 (2 ½ x ¾-inch) fluted round tart pans (about 35 grams each), and shape into balls. Press 1 dough ball into bottom and up sides of 1 prepared tart pan; trim any excess dough. Repeat with remaining dough and remaining prepared tart pans.

5. In a medium bowl, whisk together remaining 3 egg yolks (56 grams).

6. In a small saucepan, combine ¼ cup (60 grams) water, granulated sugar, evaporated milk, remaining ½ teaspoon (2 grams) vanilla, and remaining ¼ teaspoon salt. Cook over medium heat until mixture is steaming and sugar dissolves. Gradually whisk sugar mixture into egg yolks until well combined.

7. Position oven rack in lower third of oven. Preheat oven to 400°F (200°C).

8. Place a fine-mesh sieve over a large liquid-measuring cup or widemouthed pitcher. Strain egg yolk mixture through prepared sieve; discard any solids. Divide strained mixture among prepared crusts (about 18 grams each).

9. Bake until crust is lightly browned, 10 to 12 minutes, rotating pans halfway through baking. Reduce oven temperature to 350°F (180°C). Bake just until edges of filling start to puff, about 5 minutes more. Open oven door about 2 inches; bake until filling is set, a wooden pick inserted in center stands up straight, and an instant-read thermometer inserted in center registers at least 175°F (79°C), 5 to 7 minutes more. Let cool in pans for 15 minutes. Serve warm or at room temperature.

APPELTAART

Makes 1 (9-inch) pie

Inspired by the world-famous appeltaart at Amsterdam's Winkel 43, this recipe is everything an appeltaart should be: a buttery, tender crust brimming with sizeable pieces of aromatic spiced apple. Baking the apple chunks before assembling ensures a hefty filling with height while preventing a soggy bottom.

1½	cups (340 grams) unsalted butter, softened
1¾	cups (350 grams) plus 1 teaspoon (4 grams) granulated sugar, divided
¼	cup (55 grams) firmly packed light brown sugar
2	large eggs (100 grams), room temperature
1	large egg (50 grams), separated, room temperature
1	tablespoon (14 grams) vanilla bean paste
3¾	cups (469 grams) all-purpose flour
1½	teaspoons (7.5 grams) baking powder
1¼	teaspoons (3 grams) kosher salt, divided
½	teaspoon (2.5 grams) baking soda
6	large Honeycrisp apples (1,377 grams)
2	large Pink Lady apples (484 grams)
⅓	cup (43 grams) cornstarch
2	tablespoons (12 grams) ground cinnamon
2	tablespoons (6 grams) lemon zest
1	tablespoon (15 grams) fresh lemon juice

Whipped cream, to serve

1. In the bowl of a stand mixer fitted with the paddle attachment, beat butter, 1¼ cups (250 grams) granulated sugar, and brown sugar at low speed just until combined. Increase mixer speed to medium, and beat until fluffy, about 3 minutes, stopping to scrape sides of bowl. Add eggs and egg yolk, one at a time, beating until well combined after each addition. Beat in vanilla bean paste.

2. In a large bowl, whisk together flour, baking powder, 1 teaspoon (3 grams) salt, and baking soda. With mixer on low speed, gradually add flour mixture to butter mixture, beating just until combined.

Shape about two-thirds of dough (about 763 grams) into a 7-inch disk; wrap in plastic wrap. Divide remaining dough in half; shape each into a 4-inch disk. Wrap each disk in plastic wrap, and refrigerate for at least 2 hours.

3. Preheat oven to 350°F (180°C). Line 2 rimmed baking sheets with parchment paper.

4. Core apples; cut into 1- to 1½-inch chunks.

5. In a very large bowl, whisk together ½ cup (100 grams) granulated sugar, cornstarch, cinnamon, lemon zest, and remaining ¼ teaspoon salt; add apples and lemon juice, tossing to coat thoroughly. Divide apples evenly between prepared pans.

6. Bake until apples appear slightly dried, golden, and tender, 25 to 30 minutes, stirring apples and rotating pans halfway through baking. Let apples cool completely on pans, about 30 minutes. Transfer to a large bowl. Leave oven on.

7. Let dough stand at room temperature until slightly softened, 15 to 20 minutes. On a heavily floured surface, roll 7-inch dough disk into a 13-inch circle (about ¼ inch thick).

8. Spray a light-colored 9-inch springform pan with baking spray with flour. Line bottom of pan with parchment paper.

9. Using a 9-inch round cake pan or plate as a guide, cut a circle in center of rolled dough; gently transfer to prepared pan, pressing into bottom. (It's OK if dough tears while transferring; gently move to pan, and press together.) Cut remaining rolled dough into 4 pieces; gently transfer to prepared pan, overlapping if needed, pressing all the way up sides, and sealing any seams with bottom. Trim dough flush with top edge of pan; fill with cooled apple mixture.

10. On a heavily floured surface, roll remaining dough disks into 2 (9-inch) circles. Using a pastry wheel or pizza cutter, cut 1 circle into 3 (3-inch-wide) strips. Gently place strips parallel and spaced ¼ inch apart on apple mixture. Repeat with remaining dough circle, arranging strips on and perpendicular to first set of strips. Trim dough flush with edge of pan. Brush dough with egg white; sprinkle with remaining 1 teaspoon (4 grams) granulated sugar.

11. Bake until top is golden brown and slightly puffed, about 1 hour, rotating pan halfway through baking and loosely covering with foil to prevent excess browning, if necessary. Let cool in pan for 10 minutes. Carefully remove sides of pan, and let cool completely on base of pan on a wire rack. Serve with whipped cream.

Transfer dough pieces to pan. Press overlapping seams together to seal and create an even surface. It's OK if dough tears while transferring. You can press together once it's in pan.

After you've filled crust with cooled apple mixture, place dough strips parallel and spaced ¼ inch apart on apple mixture. Repeat with remaining strips, arranging on and perpendicular to first set of strips.

Trim dough flush with edge of pan. Brush dough with egg white; sprinkle with remaining granulated sugar.

SPICED PLUM LINZER TORTE

Makes 1 (9½-inch) tart

Named after the city of Linz, Austria, the Linzer torte is a classic European pastry usually served during Christmas. Traditionally made with a buttery shortcrust dough accented by ground nuts, the Linzer torte often hides a jewel-toned jam filling beneath an elaborate lattice crust. We followed sweet tradition to a T, gently arranging a hazelnut flour and almond flour crust over a beautiful plum preserves filling.

1½ cups (188 grams) all-purpose flour
1¼ cups (120 grams) finely ground hazelnut flour
1   cup (96 grams) superfine blanched almond flour
⅓   cup (67 grams) granulated sugar
⅓   cup (73 grams) firmly packed light brown sugar
1   teaspoon (3 grams) tightly packed orange zest
¾   teaspoon (2.25 grams) kosher salt
¾   teaspoon (1.5 grams) ground cinnamon
½   teaspoon (2.5 grams) baking powder
¼   teaspoon ground ginger
⅛   teaspoon ground nutmeg
⅛   teaspoon ground cloves
¾   cup plus 2 tablespoons (198 grams) cold unsalted butter, cubed
1   large egg (50 grams)
1   teaspoon (6 grams) vanilla bean paste
2   cups (600 grams) damson plum preserves
Confectioners' sugar, for dusting

1. In the work bowl of a food processor, combine flours, granulated sugar, brown sugar, orange zest, salt, cinnamon, baking powder, ginger, nutmeg, and cloves; pulse until well combined, stopping to scrape sides of bowl. Add cold butter, and pulse until mixture resembles coarse crumbs. Add egg and vanilla bean paste; pulse just until dough comes together, stopping to scrape sides of bowl. (Mixture should be moist but not sticky and should hold together when pinched.) Turn out dough onto a clean surface; reserve one-third of dough (about 264 grams), and cover with plastic wrap.
2. Spray a 9½-inch fluted round removable-bottom tart pan with baking spray with flour. Press remaining dough into bottom and up sides of prepared pan, trimming any excess with a small sharp knife; add any dough trimmings to reserved one-third of dough. Cover with plastic wrap.

3. Lightly flour a sheet of wax paper; place reserved dough on prepared wax paper, and lightly flour top of dough. Place another sheet of wax paper on dough, and roll dough into a 12-inch circle (about ⅛ inch thick); place on a baking sheet. Refrigerate rolled dough and dough in pan for 1 hour.
4. Preheat oven to 350°F (180°C).
5. Using a small offset spatula, spread preserves evenly onto dough in pan.
6. Remove top wax paper from rolled dough; using a pastry wheel or pizza cutter, cut dough into 1-inch-wide strips; cover and refrigerate until firm, about 15 minutes.
7. Gently arrange strips about ½ inch apart in a lattice pattern on preserves; press strips into edges of dough in pan, trimming off excess to create a clean edge. (If dough becomes too soft, refrigerate in 15-minute intervals as needed; a lightly floured large offset spatula can help move strips.) Create additional strips as needed by rerolling excess dough to ⅛-inch thickness between lightly floured sheets of wax paper. (This is a delicate dough. If it tears while moving, simply press it back together; alternatively, reroll, cut, and refrigerate dough, and try again.) Refrigerate assembled tart for 20 minutes.
8. Bake until crust is golden brown and set and filling is starting to bubble, 30 to 35 minutes. Let cool completely in pan on a wire rack. Remove from pan. Dust with confectioners' sugar just before serving.

BANOFFEE PIE

Makes 1 (9-inch) pie

This British pie import has been thoroughly absorbed into American tradition. With the winning combination of ripe bananas, sticky toffee, and whipped cream, it's not hard to see why.

1½ cups (195 grams) graham cracker crumbs
4½ tablespoons (54 grams) granulated sugar
¼ teaspoon kosher salt
6 to 8 tablespoons (84 to 112 grams) unsalted butter, melted
Brown Sugar Filling (recipe follows)
5 bananas (620 grams), sliced
1 tablespoon (15 grams) fresh lemon juice
Whipped Cream (recipe follows)
Garnish: chocolate shavings

1. Preheat oven to 350°F (180°C). Butter and flour a 9-inch pie plate.
2. In a medium bowl, stir together graham cracker crumbs, sugar, and salt. Add 6 tablespoons (84 grams) melted butter, and stir with a fork until moistened. Add remaining 2 tablespoons (28 grams) melted butter, if needed. Using a measuring cup, press mixture into bottom and up sides of prepared plate.
3. Bake until lightly browned, 10 to 12 minutes. Let cool on a wire rack.
4. Reserve ¼ cup Brown Sugar Filling. Pour remaining Brown Sugar Filling into prepared crust. Lightly cover with plastic wrap, and refrigerate until set, 3 to 4 hours.
5. In a medium bowl, toss together banana slices and lemon juice. Spoon bananas over chilled Brown Sugar Filling. Gently spread Whipped Cream over bananas.
6. In a small microwave-safe bowl, heat reserved ¼ cup Brown Sugar Filling on low just until pourable, about 10 seconds. Drizzle over pie. Serve immediately, or refrigerate for up to 1 hour. Garnish with chocolate shavings, if desired.

BROWN SUGAR FILLING
Makes about 2 cups

1 cup (227 grams) unsalted butter
¾ cup (165 grams) firmly packed dark brown sugar
⅔ cup (160 grams) heavy whipping cream
1 tablespoon (21 grams) light corn syrup
¼ teaspoon kosher salt

1. In a large saucepan, bring butter, brown sugar, cream, corn syrup, and salt to a boil over medium-high heat, stirring occasionally. Reduce heat to medium-low; simmer for 10 minutes. Remove from heat. Let cool for 10 minutes, stirring occasionally.

WHIPPED CREAM
Makes about 4 cups

2 cups (480 grams) heavy whipping cream
⅓ cup plus 2 tablespoons (54 grams) confectioners' sugar

1. In the bowl of a stand mixer fitted with the whisk attachment, beat cream and confectioners' sugar at high speed just until stiff peaks form.

PEAR AND CRANBERRY KUCHEN

Makes 1 (9-inch) tart

Kuchen, the German word for "cake," can mean a number of things, depending on where you live. In North and South Dakota, the kuchen you can expect is a cross between a pie and a tart, with a pastry crust filled with a blend of seasonal fruit and, of course, custard. This historic baked good was brought over by Germanic homesteaders who settled in the Dakotas, and it has since become the state dessert of South Dakota. Our version honors its forebearers with a simple spiced shortcrust filled with a generous pour of custard and an artful arrangement of pears and cranberries.

Spiced Shortcrust Pastry (recipe follows)
2   medium Anjou pears (314 grams), peeled, halved, stemmed, and cored
2   teaspoons (10 grams) fresh lemon juice
⅔   cup (160 grams) heavy whipping cream
¼   cup (50 grams) granulated sugar
2   large egg yolks (37 grams)
⅛   teaspoon kosher salt
⅛   teaspoon ground cinnamon
⅛   teaspoon ground ginger
⅛   teaspoon ground cloves
¾   cup (83 grams) fresh or frozen cranberries
Garnish: confectioners' sugar, apricot preserves

1. Preheat oven to 400°F (200°C).
2. Top prepared Spiced Shortcrust Pastry with a piece of parchment paper, letting ends extend over edges of pan. Add pie weights.
3. Bake until edges look dry, about 15 minutes. Carefully remove parchment and weights. Bake until bottom crust looks dry, about 5 minutes more. Reduce oven temperature to 300°F (150°C).
4. Slice each pear half lengthwise into ¼-inch-thick slices. Working with one half at a time, slide pieces into a line, and place, evenly spaced, in a line in prepared crust. Brush lemon juice all over pears.
5. In a small bowl, whisk together cream, granulated sugar, egg yolks, salt, cinnamon, ginger, and cloves. Pour mixture between pears in crust; sprinkle cranberries on top.

6. Bake until edges are set, center jiggles slightly, and an instant-read thermometer inserted in center registers 170°F (77°C) to 175°F (79°C), 40 to 50 minutes. Let cool completely in pan on a wire rack. Serve immediately, or refrigerate until ready to serve. Just before serving, place an 8-inch circle of parchment paper in center of tart, and dust confectioners' sugar onto outside edge, if desired. Brush pears with apricot preserves, if desired. Serve chilled or at room temperature.

SPICED SHORTCRUST PASTRY
Makes 1 (9-inch) crust

1¾   cups (219 grams) all-purpose flour
⅓   cup (67 grams) granulated sugar
½   teaspoon (1.5 grams) kosher salt
½   teaspoon (1 gram) ground cinnamon
½   teaspoon (1 gram) ground ginger
¼   teaspoon (1.25 grams) baking powder
¼   teaspoon ground cloves
½   cup (113 grams) cold unsalted butter, cubed
1   large egg (50 grams), lightly beaten
1   tablespoon (15 grams) heavy whipping cream

1. Spray a 9-inch fluted round removable-bottom tart pan with cooking spray.
2. In the bowl of a stand mixer fitted with the paddle attachment, beat flour, sugar, salt, cinnamon, ginger, baking powder, and cloves at low speed until combined. Add cold butter, and beat until mixture is crumbly and resembles fine bread crumbs and no large pieces of butter remain, 2 to 3 minutes. Add egg and cream, and beat at low speed until a dough forms. Press dough into bottom and up sides of prepared pan. (Alternatively, on a lightly floured surface, roll dough into an 11-inch circle [about ¼ inch thick]; transfer to prepared pan, pressing into bottom and up sides.) Trim excess dough, and discard. Using a fork, prick bottom of dough all over. Freeze until firm, 10 to 15 minutes.

PECAN BUTTER TARTS

Makes 12 mini tarts

Recipe by Emily Turner

While much of Canada's cuisine has European roots and inspiration, butter tarts, which first appeared in Ontario in the early 1900s, are uniquely Canadian. Some insist that the only authentic filling must include raisins, but we'll let you be the judge of that.

Flaky Pastry Dough (recipe follows)
¾   cup (165 grams) firmly packed light brown sugar
5   tablespoons (70 grams) unsalted butter, melted
¼   cup (85 grams) dark corn syrup
¼   cup (85 grams) Grade A amber maple syrup
2   large eggs (100 grams)
1½   teaspoons (6 grams) vanilla extract
1   teaspoon (5 grams) distilled white vinegar
¼   teaspoon kosher salt
½   cup (57 grams) chopped pecans

1. Preheat oven to 450°F (230°C). Butter and flour a 12-cup muffin pan.
2. On a lightly floured surface, roll half of Flaky Pastry Dough to ⅛-inch thickness. Using a 4½- to 5-inch round cutter, cut dough into 6 circles, rerolling scraps once. Gently press rounds into prepared muffin cups, letting edges fold up around each other and extend over sides of pan. Repeat with remaining dough. Freeze for 20 minutes.
3. In a medium bowl, whisk together brown sugar, melted butter, corn syrup, maple syrup, eggs, vanilla, vinegar, and salt. Spoon 2 to 2½ teaspoons (4 to 5 grams) pecans into each prepared crust. Pour filling on top of pecans to ½ inch below edge of crust.
4. Bake in bottom third of oven for 10 minutes. Reduce oven temperature to 400°F (200°C). Bake until filling is set and puffed, 8 to 10 minutes more, covering with foil to prevent excess browning, if necessary. (If you want a runnier texture to your butter tart, bake just until filling is set, 3 to 4 minutes less.) Let cool in pan for 10 minutes. Run a sharp knife around edges of tarts, and let cool completely in pan. (If you have difficulty removing tarts from pan, freeze for 20 minutes before popping them out.) Bring to room temperature before serving.

FLAKY PASTRY DOUGH

Makes dough for 12 mini tarts

3½   cups (438 grams) all-purpose flour
1   tablespoon (12 grams) granulated sugar
1   teaspoon (3 grams) kosher salt
½   cup (113 grams) cold all-vegetable shortening, cubed
½   cup (113 grams) cold unsalted butter, cubed
5 to 8 tablespoons (75 to 120 grams) cold water, divided
1   large egg yolk (19 grams)
1½   teaspoons (7.5 grams) fresh lemon juice

1. In the work bowl of a food processor, place flour, sugar, and salt; pulse until combined. Add cold shortening and butter, and pulse until mixture is crumbly.
2. In a small bowl, whisk together ⅓ cup (80 grams) cold water, egg yolk, and lemon juice. With processor running, gradually add egg yolk mixture, pulsing until dough begins to come together. (Dough will be softer than a pie dough, but you don't want it to be sticky.) Add remaining water, if necessary.
3. Turn out dough onto a lightly floured surface, and knead until dough comes together. Divide in half. On a lightly floured sheet of parchment paper, roll half of dough to ¼-inch thickness. Transfer to a parchment-lined rimmed baking sheet. Repeat with remaining dough; transfer to a separate parchment-lined rimmed baking sheet. Cover and refrigerate for 1 hour.

Photo by Maya Visnyei

RETRO
REVAMPS

BLUEBERRY PIE MEETS LEMON MERINGUE IN A MARRIAGE
OF SWEET AND TART, AND CREAMY SWEET POTATO PIE
GETS A MOUNTAIN OF CRUNCHY CANDIED PECANS IN THIS
REDUX RECIPE CHAPTER

BLACK BOTTOM COCONUT CREAM TART

Makes 1 (14x4-inch) tart

Tall peaks of toasted marshmallow fluff hide Coconut Pastry Cream and ganache.

1   cup (227 grams) unsalted butter, softened
¾   cup (165 grams) firmly packed brown sugar
2   tablespoons (42 grams) honey
1   tablespoon (21 grams) molasses
1   teaspoon (3 grams) kosher salt
1   teaspoon (2 grams) ground cinnamon
2   cups (260 grams) whole wheat flour
1   cup (125 grams) all-purpose flour
1   teaspoon (5 grams) baking soda
Ganache Filling (recipe follows)
Coconut Pastry Cream (recipe follows)
Fluffy Marshmallow Cream (recipe follows)

1. Spray a 14x4-inch removable-bottom tart pan with cooking spray.
2. In the bowl of a stand mixer fitted with the paddle attachment, beat butter, brown sugar, honey, molasses, salt, and cinnamon at medium speed until combined. In a small bowl, whisk together all-purpose flour and baking soda. Gradually add whole wheat flour to butter mixture alternately with all-purpose flour mixture, beating until combined.
3. Preheat oven to 315°F (157°C).
4. Roll dough into a 15x5-inch rectangle. Transfer to prepared pan, pressing into bottom and up sides. Prick bottom and sides of dough with a fork.
5. Bake for 15 minutes. Let cool completely.
6. Pour Ganache Filling into prepared crust; refrigerate until firm. Spread Coconut Pastry Cream over ganache layer. Using an offset spatula, swirl Fluffy Marshmallow Cream onto tart. Using a kitchen torch, brown meringue. Refrigerate for up to 2 days.

GANACHE FILLING
Makes 1 cup

⅔   cup (113 grams) 60% cacao semisweet chocolate morsels
⅓   cup (80 grams) heavy whipping cream
1   tablespoon (21 grams) light corn syrup
½   teaspoon (2 grams) vanilla extract
¼   teaspoon kosher salt

1. Place chocolate in a medium bowl, and set aside.
2. In a small saucepan, bring cream and corn syrup to a simmer over medium-low heat; pour over chocolate. Let stand for 2 minutes. Whisk mixture, starting from the center and working outward, until smooth. Add vanilla and salt, and whisk until combined.

COCONUT PASTRY CREAM
Makes 1½ cups

¼   cup (50 grams) granulated sugar
1½   tablespoons (12 grams) cornstarch
⅛   teaspoon kosher salt
½   cup (120 grams) whole milk
½   cup (120 grams) unsweetened full-fat coconut milk
2   large egg yolks (37 grams)
½   cup (42 grams) sweetened flaked coconut

1. Line a large rimmed baking sheet with plastic wrap.
2. In a medium saucepan, combine sugar, cornstarch, and salt. Whisk in milk, coconut milk, and egg yolks. Cook over medium heat, stirring constantly, until thickened, about 10 minutes. Remove from heat, and stir in coconut.
3. Pour hot coconut mixture onto prepared pan. Top with another piece of plastic wrap, making sure entire surface is touching plastic wrap. Refrigerate for at least 2 hours or overnight.

FLUFFY MARSHMALLOW CREAM
Makes 4 cups

3   large egg whites (90 grams)
½   teaspoon (1 gram) cream of tartar
⅔   cup (133 grams) plus 2 tablespoons (24 grams) granulated sugar, divided
¾   cup (255 grams) light corn syrup
⅓   cup (80 grams) water
2   teaspoons (12 grams) vanilla bean paste

1. In the bowl of a stand mixer fitted with the whisk attachment, beat egg whites and cream of tartar at medium speed until foamy. Add 2 tablespoons (24 grams) sugar, and beat until soft peaks form.
2. In a medium saucepan, combine corn syrup, ⅓ cup (80 grams) water, and remaining ⅔ cup (133 grams) sugar. Cook over medium heat, stirring constantly, until mixture registers 248°F (120°C) on a candy thermometer, about 15 minutes.
3. With mixer on medium speed, pour corn syrup mixture into egg white mixture in a slow, steady stream until combined. Increase mixer speed to high, and beat for 5 minutes. Add vanilla bean paste, and beat for 1 minute.

ORANGE BLOSSOM VANILLA BROWN SUGAR PIE

Makes 1 (10-inch) pie

Orange blossom water offers light, floral flavor while a crisp brûlée topping lends a crunchy texture to the custard filling in this elegant pie.

2¾ cups (330 grams) crushed shortbread cookies
½ cup (110 grams) firmly packed light brown sugar
6 tablespoons (84 grams) unsalted butter, melted
1 teaspoon (2 grams) orange zest
⅛ teaspoon kosher salt
Orange Blossom Filling (recipe follows)
3 tablespoons (36 grams) granulated sugar
3 tablespoons (36 grams) turbinado sugar

1. Preheat oven to 350°F (180°C).
2. In a medium bowl, stir together crushed cookies, brown sugar, melted butter, zest, and salt. Using a measuring cup, press mixture into bottom and up sides of a 10-inch pie plate.
3. Bake until golden brown, about 15 minutes. Let cool completely on a wire rack.
4. Pour Orange Blossom Filling into prepared crust. Cover and refrigerate for at least 1 hour. Refrigerate for at least 1 hour. In a small bowl, stir together granulated sugar and turbinado sugar. Sprinkle sugar mixture over filling. Use a kitchen torch to brûlée top.

Orange Blossom Filling

Makes 2½ cups

1 cup (240 grams) whole milk
1¾ cups (420 grams) heavy whipping cream, divided
⅔ cup (147 grams) firmly packed light brown sugar, divided
¼ teaspoon kosher salt
4½ tablespoons (36 grams) cornstarch
5 large egg yolks (93 grams)
2 teaspoons (12 grams) vanilla bean paste, divided
2 tablespoons (28 grams) unsalted butter, softened
1 tablespoon (13 grams) orange blossom water

1. In a medium saucepan, bring milk, 1 cup (240 grams) cream, ⅓ cup (73.5 grams) brown sugar, and salt to a boil over medium heat.
2. In a medium bowl, whisk together cornstarch, egg yolks, 1 teaspoon (6 grams) vanilla bean paste, and remaining ⅓ cup (73.5 grams) brown sugar. Whisking constantly, pour hot milk mixture into egg mixture. Return milk mixture to saucepan, and cook, stirring constantly, until a instant-read thermometer registers 180°F (82°C). Remove from heat, and whisk in butter and orange blossom water.
3. Strain mixture over a rimmed baking sheet lined with plastic wrap. Press another piece of plastic wrap directly onto surface of pastry cream. Place baking pan on a wire rack, and let cool to room temperature.
4. Transfer pastry cream to the bowl of a stand mixer fitted with the paddle attachment, and beat at medium speed until smooth. Transfer to a large bowl; set aside.
5. Clean bowl of stand mixer. Using the whisk attachment, beat remaining ¾ cup (180 grams) cream and remaining 1 teaspoon (6 grams) vanilla bean paste at high speed until soft peaks form. Fold whipped cream into pastry cream until combined and smooth. Use immediately.

BUTTERNUT SQUASH PIE

Makes 1 (9-inch) pie

Forget pumpkin and sweet potato. This bourbon-spiked squash pie is the star of your next holiday dinner. This pie embodies all that a custard pie should be, appearing firm with clean slices, but dissolving into silky deliciousness with every bite.

⅔   cup (147 grams) firmly packed light brown sugar
2   large eggs (100 grams)
1   large egg yolk (19 grams)
2   tablespoons (30 grams) bourbon
1   teaspoon (2 grams) ground ginger
1   teaspoon (4 grams) vanilla extract
¾   teaspoon (1.5 grams) ground cinnamon
½   teaspoon (1.5 grams) kosher salt
½   teaspoon (1 gram) smoked paprika
1   cup (244 grams) roasted butternut squash purée*
¾   cup (180 grams) heavy whipping cream
Rosemary Saltine Crumb Crust (recipe follows)
Garnish: Maple Whipped Cream (recipe follows)

1. Preheat oven to 325°F (170°C).
2. In a medium bowl, whisk together brown sugar, eggs, egg yolk, bourbon, ginger, vanilla, cinnamon, salt, and paprika. Add squash purée, and whisk until well combined. Whisking constantly, slowly pour in cream until well combined. Transfer mixture to prepared Rosemary Saltine Crumb Crust.
3. Bake until edges are set and center is still slightly jiggly, 45 to 55 minutes, covering crust with foil after 20 minutes of baking to prevent excess browning, if necessary. Let cool completely on a wire rack. Garnish with Maple Whipped Cream, if desired.

*To make butternut squash purée, coat 1 peeled, seeded, and quartered butternut squash with 1 tablespoon (14 grams) olive oil. Place on a baking sheet lined with parchment paper. Roast in a 400°F (200°C) oven until soft, 45 minutes to 1 hour. Let cool completely. Scrape out pulp. Transfer pulp to the work bowl of a food processor; process on high until puréed. Refrigerate for up to 5 days.

ROSEMARY SALTINE CRUMB CRUST

Makes 1 (9-inch) crust

The savory herbs and salty notes in this cracker-based crumb crust complement the fragrant spices in this pie's filling. We love the brighter, gold crust that saltines create and how it makes the burnt orange in the filling pop, encircling it like a crumbly halo.

2   cups (154 grams) saltine cracker crumbs
⅓   cup (73 grams) firmly packed light brown sugar
1   tablespoon (2 grams) chopped fresh rosemary
½   cup (113 grams) unsalted butter, melted

1. Preheat oven to 350°F (180°C).
2. In a medium bowl, whisk together cracker crumbs, brown sugar, and rosemary. Add melted butter, and whisk to combine. Using the bottom of a measuring cup, gently press crumb mixture into bottom and up sides of a 9-inch pie plate.
3. Bake until lightly golden brown and set, about 15 minutes. Let cool completely.

MAPLE WHIPPED CREAM

Makes about 1½ cups

This whipped cream is the perfect sweet topping to any dessert.

½   cup (120 grams) heavy whipping cream
2   tablespoons (42 grams) maple syrup

1. In the bowl of a stand mixer fitted with the whisk attachment, beat cream and maple syrup at high speed until stiff peaks form, 2 to 3 minutes. Refrigerate for up to 24 hours.

ICEBOX KEY LIME PIE

Makes 1 (9-inch) deep-dish pie

Classic Key lime pie gets a spicy upgrade with our Gingersnap Crust flecked with crystallized ginger.

1½ cups (360 grams) coconut cream
½   cup (120 grams) Key lime juice (from bottle)
8   ounces (225 grams) cream cheese, softened
1   cup (120 grams) confectioners' sugar
½   cup (120 grams) crème fraîche
¾   cup (180 grams) heavy whipping cream
Gingersnap Crust (recipe follows)
Garnish: lime slices

1. In a small bowl, whisk together coconut cream and Key lime juice; set aside.
2. In the bowl of a stand mixer fitted with the paddle attachment, beat cream cheese at medium-high speed until creamy, about 3 minutes. Add confectioners' sugar and crème fraîche, beating until smooth. With mixer on low speed, add coconut cream mixture, beating to combine. Transfer to a large bowl; set aside.
3. Using the whisk attachment, beat heavy cream at medium-high speed until stiff peaks form. Add one-third of whipped heavy cream to cream cheese mixture, and whisk until smooth. Whisk in remaining whipped heavy cream. Spoon mixture into prepared Gingersnap Crust until mixture is even with top of crust. Freeze for at least 4 hours or overnight. Let stand at room temperature for 15 minutes before serving. Garnish with limes, if desired.

GINGERSNAP CRUST
Makes 1 (9-inch) deep-dish crust

2¾ cups (358 grams) ground gingersnap cookies
¼   cup plus 3 tablespoons (99 grams) unsalted butter, melted
3   tablespoons (42 grams) firmly packed light brown sugar
3   tablespoons (33 grams) finely chopped crystallized ginger

1. Preheat oven to 350°F (180°C).
2. In a medium bowl, stir together all ingredients. Firmly press mixture into bottom and completely up sides of a 9-inch deep-dish pie plate.
3. Bake until set and fragrant, 10 to 12 minutes. Let cool completely.

MEYER LEMON SHAKER PIE

Makes 1 (9-inch) pie

Originally thought up by the Shaker community in the Midwest, Shaker pie is made up of whole slices of macerated lemons and a rustic, flaky crust. We twirled up the traditional recipe by using Meyer lemons for our filling. The maceration process releases the Meyers' subtle floral quality while our Ginger Pie Dough balances out the filling's tart flavor with a sweet and spicy kick.

2   large Meyer lemons (349 grams)
1¾ cups (350 grams) granulated sugar
¼   cup (55 grams) firmly packed light brown sugar
½   teaspoon (1.5 grams) kosher salt
Ginger Pie Dough (recipe follows)
3   tablespoons (24 grams) all-purpose flour
¼   teaspoon ground cinnamon
⅛   teaspoon ground nutmeg
4   large eggs (200 grams), lightly beaten
¼   cup (57 grams) unsalted butter, melted
1   large egg white (30 grams), lightly beaten
1   tablespoon (15 grams) water
Sparkling sugar, for sprinkling

1. Using a serrated knife, cut lemons crosswise into ⅛- to 1/16-inch-thick slices, discarding ends and seeds. Coarsely chop lemon slices into ½- to ¾-inch pieces, and place in a large bowl with any juices. Stir in granulated sugar, brown sugar, and salt; cover and let stand at room temperature, stirring occasionally, for 4 hours or up to overnight.
2. Preheat oven to 425°F (220°C).
3. Let Ginger Pie Dough stand at room temperature until slightly softened, 15 to 20 minutes. On a lightly floured surface, roll half of dough into a 12-inch circle (about ⅛ inch thick). Press into bottom and up sides of a 9-inch pie plate.
4. In a medium bowl, whisk together flour, cinnamon, and nutmeg. Add eggs and melted butter, whisking until well combined. Add flour mixture to lemon mixture, stirring until well combined; pour into prepared crust.

5. In a small bowl, whisk together egg white and 1 tablespoon (15 grams) water. Brush dough edges with egg wash.
6. On a lightly floured surface, roll remaining dough into a 12-inch circle. Carefully place over filling; trim dough to ½- to 1-inch overhang. Fold edges under, and crimp, if desired. Brush dough with egg wash; sprinkle with sparkling sugar. Using a sharp knife, cut 8 slits in top to vent.
7. Bake for 25 minutes, covering edges with foil to prevent excess browning and re-cutting slits in top, if necessary. Reduce oven temperature to 350°F (180°C). Bake until crust is golden brown, 20 to 25 minutes more. Let cool completely before serving.

GINGER PIE DOUGH
Makes 1 (9-inch) double crust

3   cups (375 grams) all-purpose flour
3   tablespoons (36 grams) granulated sugar
2   teaspoons (4 grams) ground ginger
1¾ teaspoons (5.25 grams) kosher salt
1   cup (227 grams) cold unsalted butter, cubed
6   tablespoons (90 grams) ice water

1. In the work bowl of a food processor, place flour, sugar, ginger, and salt; pulse until combined, about 4 times. Add cold butter; pulse until butter is pea-size. Add 6 tablespoons (90 grams) ice water; pulse until dough forms large clumps.
2. Turn out dough onto a lightly floured surface. Divide in half, and shape into disks. Wrap tightly in plastic wrap, and refrigerate for at least 1 hour.

SPICED HONEY-OAT PIE

Makes 1 (9-inch) pie

This richly spiced oat pie is a nut-free take on the classic pecan pie, inspired by a brilliant recipe by Southern Baked Pie Company founder Amanda Wilbanks. A gooey oat-packed filling is poured into an aromatic cinnamon piecrust and baked to golden perfection.

Cinnamon Pie Dough (recipe follows)
1⅓ cups (125 grams) old-fashioned oats
⅔ cup (147 grams) firmly packed light brown sugar
1¼ teaspoons (3.75 grams) kosher salt
¼ teaspoon ground ginger
⅛ teaspoon ground nutmeg
½ cup (170 grams) light corn syrup
6 tablespoons (84 grams) unsalted butter, melted
⅓ cup (113 grams) clover honey
1½ tablespoons (19.5 grams) Irish whiskey
2 teaspoons (8 grams) vanilla extract
4 large eggs (200 grams), room temperature
Whiskey Whipped Cream (recipe follows), to serve

1. Preheat oven to 400°F (200°C).
2. Let Cinnamon Pie Dough stand at room temperature until softened, 10 to 15 minutes. On a lightly floured surface, roll dough into a 12-inch circle. Transfer to a 9-inch pie plate, pressing into bottom and up sides. Fold edges under, and crimp, if desired; freeze until firm, about 15 minutes.
3. Top Cinnamon Pie Dough with a piece of parchment paper, letting ends extend over edges of plate. Add pie weights.
4. Bake until edges are lightly golden, 10 to 15 minutes. Carefully remove parchment and weights. Bake until dry and set, about 10 minutes more, lightly covering edges with foil to prevent excess browning, if necessary. Let cool completely on a wire rack. Reduce oven temperature to 350°F (180°C).
5. Line a rimmed baking sheet with parchment paper. Place oats on prepared pan.

6. Bake until lightly toasted, about 10 minutes, stirring occasionally. Let cool completely on pan on a wire rack. Position oven rack in lower third of oven. Reduce oven temperature to 325°F (170°C).
7. In a large bowl, whisk together brown sugar, salt, ginger, and nutmeg. Add corn syrup, melted butter, honey, whiskey, and vanilla; whisk until well combined. Add eggs, one at a time, whisking well after each addition. Stir in toasted oats; pour filling into prepared crust.
8. Bake until filling is set and slightly puffed and an instant-read thermometer inserted in center registers 200°F (93°C), 40 to 45 minutes, loosely covering crust with foil to prevent excess browning, if necessary. Let cool completely on a wire rack. Serve with Whiskey Whipped Cream.

CINNAMON PIE DOUGH

Makes 1 (9-inch) crust

1½ cups (188 grams) all-purpose flour
1½ tablespoons (18 grams) granulated sugar
1 teaspoon (3 grams) kosher salt
¾ teaspoon (1.5 grams) ground cinnamon
½ cup (113 grams) cold unsalted butter, cubed
3 tablespoons (45 grams) ice water

1. In the work bowl of a food processor, place flour, sugar, salt, and cinnamon; pulse until combined, about 4 times. Add cold butter; pulse until butter is almond-size. Pour 3 tablespoons (45 grams) ice water through food chute in a slow, steady stream. Pulse until dough just forms a ball.
2. Turn out dough onto a lightly floured surface. Shape into a disk; wrap tightly with plastic wrap. Refrigerate for at least 1 hour.

WHISKEY WHIPPED CREAM

Makes about 2½ cups

1 cup (240 grams) cold heavy whipping cream
1½ tablespoons (19.5 grams) Irish whiskey
1 tablespoon (21 grams) clover honey

1. In the bowl of a stand mixer fitted with the whisk attachment, beat all ingredients at medium-high speed until medium-stiff peaks form. Use immediately, or cover and refrigerate until ready to serve.

APPLE CRUMB PIE

Makes 1 (9-inch) pie

Traditional apple pie gets an updo with a creamy crème fraîche custard filling. Layers upon layers of crisp sweet apples are topped with a creamy base and baked until soft. With a splash of spiced rum and a crunchy Almond Streusel topping, this recipe begs for ice cream.

1¼ pounds (567 grams) ¼-inch-sliced Honeycrisp apple (about 5½ cups)
1¼ pounds (567 grams) ¼-inch-sliced Pink Lady apple (about 5½ cups)
¾   cup (150 grams) granulated sugar, divided
2   tablespoons (30 grams) spiced rum, divided
1   tablespoon (15 grams) fresh lemon juice
¾   teaspoon (1.5 grams) kosher salt, divided
All-Butter Pie Dough (recipe follows)
1⅓ cups (320 grams) crème fraîche
1   large egg (50 grams), room temperature
3   tablespoons (24 grams) all-purpose flour
1   teaspoon (6 grams) vanilla bean paste
Almond Streusel (recipe follows)
Garnish: confectioners' sugar

1. Preheat oven to 400°F (200°C). Line 2 rimmed baking sheets with parchment paper.
2. In a very large bowl, stir together apple slices, ¼ cup (50 grams) granulated sugar, 1 tablespoon (15 grams) rum, lemon juice, and ¼ teaspoon salt until well combined. Let stand for 15 minutes. Divide apple mixture between prepared pans, spreading into an even layer.
3. Bake until apples are fork-tender and have released significant moisture, 20 to 26 minutes, rotating pans and stirring mixture halfway through baking. (Apples will be slightly reduced in size but still retain their shape.) Let cool on pans on wire racks. Leave oven on.
4. Let All-Butter Pie Dough stand at room temperature until slightly softened, 10 to 15 minutes. On a lightly floured surface, roll dough into a 14-inch circle (about ⅛ inch thick). Transfer to a 9-inch deep-dish pie plate, pressing into bottom and up sides. Trim dough to ½ inch beyond edge of plate; fold edges under, and crimp, if desired. Freeze until firm, about 20 minutes.
5. Top dough with parchment paper; add pie weights. Place on a baking sheet.
6. Bake until edges of crust are lightly golden and just set, 15 to 20 minutes. Carefully remove weights and parchment; bake until inside of crust is dry and just set, 8 to 10 minutes, lightly covering edges of crust with foil to prevent excess browning, if necessary. Let cool completely on pan on a wire rack. Position oven rack in bottom third of oven. Reduce oven temperature to 350°F (180°C).
7. In another very large bowl, whisk together crème fraîche, egg, flour, vanilla bean paste, remaining ½ cup (100 grams) granulated sugar, remaining 1 tablespoon (15 grams) rum, and remaining ½ teaspoon (1.5 grams) salt. Fold in cooled apple mixture until thoroughly coated; pour into prepared crust, spreading into an even layer.
8. Bake until filling edges are just starting to set but mixture is still jiggly, about 25 minutes, lightly covering crust with foil to prevent

excess browning, if necessary. Sprinkle Almond Streusel evenly over filling. Bake until streusel is lightly golden, apples are tender, filling is slightly puffed and set, and an instant-read thermometer inserted in center registers at least 162°F (72°C), 35 to 40 minutes more, lightly covering crust with foil to prevent excess browning, if necessary. Let cool completely on a wire rack before slicing, or refrigerate until ready to serve. Garnish with confectioners' sugar, if desired.

ALL-BUTTER PIE DOUGH
Makes 1 (9-inch) deep-dish crust

2   cups (250 grams) all-purpose flour
2   tablespoons (24 grams) granulated sugar
1½ teaspoons (4.5 grams) kosher salt
10 tablespoons (140 grams) cold unsalted butter, cut into ½- to ¾-inch cubes
¼   cup (60 grams) ice water

1. In the work bowl of a food processor, place flour, sugar, and salt; pulse until combined. Add cold butter; pulse until butter is pea-size. (If any large pieces of butter remain, squeeze between fingers to break up.) Gradually add ¼ cup (60 grams) ice water, 1 tablespoon (15 grams) at a time, pulsing 2 to 3 times to combine before adding next addition. Pulse just until moist crumbs that hold together when pressed form, stopping to scrape sides of bowl.
2. Turn out dough onto a work surface. Press together until a cohesive dough is formed. Shape into a 6-inch disk, and wrap in plastic wrap. Refrigerate for at least 1 hour.

ALMOND STREUSEL
Makes about 3 cups

⅓   cup (42 grams) all-purpose flour
3   tablespoons (36 grams) granulated sugar
¼   teaspoon kosher salt
¼   teaspoon ground cinnamon
¼   cup (57 grams) unsalted butter, melted and cooled for 10 minutes
¼   teaspoon (1.5 grams) vanilla bean paste
½   cup (46 grams) sliced almonds

1. In a medium bowl, whisk together flour, sugar, salt, and cinnamon. Add melted butter and vanilla bean paste; stir until well combined. Break up butter mixture, stir in almonds, and crumble as desired. Set aside until ready to use.

CHOCOLATE CHESS PIE

Makes 1 (9-inch) pie

Recipe by Ruth Guffey Holt

A take on classic chess pie, the simple addition of cocoa powder transforms the custard into a rich, fudgy filling. The top of the pie, crackled in appearance, has a thin layer of crisply caramelized sugar, while the inside custard appears shiny and soft when set. Each bite is sure to thrill the pie enthusiast and excite the chocolate lover.

Pie Dough (recipe follows)
1½   cups (300 grams) granulated sugar
¼   cup (21 grams) unsweetened cocoa powder, sifted
3   large eggs (150 grams), room temperature
6   tablespoons (84 grams) unsalted butter, melted and cooled to room temperature
1½   teaspoons (6 grams) vanilla extract
¾   cup (180 grams) whole buttermilk, room temperature
Sweetened whipped cream, to serve
Garnish: chocolate shavings

1. Preheat oven to 400°F (200°C).
2. On a lightly floured surface, roll Pie Dough into a 12-inch circle. Transfer to a 9-inch pie plate, pressing into bottom and up sides. Trim excess dough to ½ inch beyond edge of pan. Fold edges under, and crimp, if desired. Freeze for 15 minutes.
3. Top Pie Dough with a piece of parchment paper, letting ends extend over edges of pan. Add pie weights.
4. Bake until edges are just dry, 10 to 15 minutes. Carefully remove parchment and weights. Bake until bottom is dry and set, 2 to 5 minutes more, lightly covering edges with foil to prevent excess browning, if necessary. (Crust may puff up some, but this is normal.) Let cool completely on a wire rack, at least 20 minutes. Reduce oven temperature to 350°F (180°C).
5. In the bowl of a stand mixer fitted with the paddle attachment, beat sugar and cocoa at low speed until combined. Add eggs, melted butter, and vanilla, and beat at medium speed until combined. Add buttermilk, beating until smooth and stopping to scrape sides of bowl. Pour into prepared crust.
6. Bake until a knife inserted near edge comes out clean, 35 to 45 minutes, covering edges with foil to prevent excess browning, if necessary. Let cool completely on a wire rack. Serve with whipped cream. Garnish with chocolate shavings, if desired.

PIE DOUGH
Makes 1 (9-inch) crust

1½   cups (188 grams) all-purpose flour
1   teaspoon (3 grams) kosher salt
½   cup (113 grams) cold unsalted butter, cubed
4 to 5 tablespoons (60 to 75 grams) ice water

1. In the work bowl of a food processor, place flour and salt; pulse until combined. Add cold butter, and pulse until mixture is crumbly and butter is pea-size. With processor running, add 4 tablespoons (60 grams) ice water in a slow, steady stream just until dough comes together; add up to remaining 1 tablespoon (15 grams) water, 1 teaspoon (5 grams) at a time, if necessary. (Mixture may appear crumbly. It should be moist and hold together when pinched.)
2. Turn out dough, and shape into a disk. Wrap tightly in plastic wrap, and refrigerate for at least 1 hour. Dough may be refrigerated for up to 3 days or frozen for up to 2 months. Before using, let Pie Dough stand at room temperature until softened, 10 to 15 minutes.

[retro revamps]

BLUEBERRY LEMON MERINGUE

Makes 1 (9-inch) pie

Recipe by Erin Jeanne McDowell

Why decide between sweet, juicy blueberry pie and tart, toasty lemon meringue when you can have both?

Blueberry Filling:
3½ cups (595 grams) fresh blueberries, divided
1 tablespoon (15 grams) fresh lemon juice
½ cup (100 grams) granulated sugar, divided
¼ cup (30 grams) all-purpose flour
¼ teaspoon (1 gram) fine sea salt
1 tablespoon (14 grams) unsalted butter
1 teaspoon (5 grams) vanilla extract

All Buttah Pie Dough (recipe follows), par-baked and cooled

Lemon Curd Filling:
¾ cup (150 grams) granulated sugar
¼ cup (28 grams) cornstarch
6 tablespoons (85 grams) unsalted butter
1 cup (226 grams) fresh lemon juice (about 5 to 6 lemons)
6 large egg yolks (128 grams)
¼ teaspoon (1 gram) fine sea salt

Mile-High Meringue Topping:
4 large egg whites (142 grams)
1 cup (198 grams) granulated sugar
2 teaspoons (10 grams) vanilla extract (optional)
½ teaspoon (2 grams) cream of tartar
Large pinch fine sea salt

1. For blueberry filling: In a medium saucepan, toss together 2½ cups (495 grams) blueberries, ¼ cup (50 grams) sugar, and lemon juice. Cook over medium-low heat, stirring occasionally, until berries start to break down and become juicy, 8 to 10 minutes. Using a potato masher, coarsely mash berries a few times.
2. In a small bowl, whisk together flour, salt, and remaining ¼ cup (50 grams) sugar. Sprinkle flour mixture onto blueberry mixture, and stir

until well combined. Bring to a boil, stirring constantly, and cook for 1 minute. Turn off heat, and stir in butter and vanilla.
3. Using an immersion blender, purée blueberry mixture until relatively smooth. (Alternatively, transfer to a blender or food processor, and process until relatively smooth.) Stir in remaining 1 cup (170 grams) blueberries. Let cool completely. (To cool quickly, pour blueberry filling onto a rimmed baking sheet.)
4. Preheat oven to 400°F (200°C).
5. On a parchment paper-lined baking sheet, place par-baked All Buttah Pie Dough crust. Pour cooled blueberry filling into prepared crust, and spread into an even layer.
6. Bake until crust is deeply golden and filling is bubbly and has a matte surface, 30 to 35 minutes. Let cool completely.
7. For lemon curd filling: In a small bowl, whisk together sugar and cornstarch until combined.
8. In a medium saucepan, melt butter over medium heat. Reduce heat to medium-low, and add sugar mixture, lemon juice, egg yolks, and salt. Cook, whisking constantly, until mixture begins to thicken, 15 to 18 minutes. Cook, stirring constantly with a silicone spatula (be sure to get into edges and corners of pot), until thickened and large bubbles begin to break surface in center of pan, 2 to 3 minutes.
9. Strain lemon curd filling through a fine-mesh sieve into cooled prepared crust, and spread into an even layer on top of blueberry filling. Cover with a piece of plastic wrap, pressing wrap directly onto surface of lemon curd filling to prevent a skin from forming. Refrigerate until completely cool, at least 4 hours or up to 24 hours.
10. For mile-high meringue topping: In the heatproof bowl of a stand mixer, whisk together egg whites, sugar, vanilla (if using), cream of tartar, and salt. Place bowl over a saucepan of simmering water, and cook, whisking constantly, until an instant-read thermometer registers 160°F (71°C).
11. Return bowl to stand mixer. Using the whisk attachment, beat at medium-high speed until stiff peaks form, 4 to 5 minutes.
12. Pile meringue on top of cooled pie. Spread meringue to edges, but keep it piled a bit higher in center. Using a handheld kitchen torch, carefully brown meringue before serving, if desired.

ALL BUTTAH PIE DOUGH
Makes 1 (9-inch) crust

This is my go-to pie dough. I learned to make pie dough using butter and shortening or lard, but when it came time to choose my one and only fat, it's all buttah, all the time. The flavor and flakiness butter gives piecrust just can't be beat. This recipe doubles (and even triples or quadruples) well if you're making a double crust pie or want additional dough for decorative effects.

1¼ cups (151 grams) all-purpose flour
¼ teaspoon (1 gram) fine sea salt
8 tablespoons (113 grams) cold unsalted butter, cut into ½-inch cubes
¼ cup (57 grams) ice water, plus more as needed

1. In a large bowl, whisk together the flour and salt. Add the cubed butter, tossing the cubes through the flour until each individual piece is well coated. "Cut" the butter into the flour by pressing the pieces between your fingers, flattening the cubes into big shards. As you work, continue to toss the butter through the flour, recoating the shingled pieces.

2. Continue cutting the butter into the flour just until the pieces of butter are about the size of walnut halves.

3. Make a well in the center of the flour mixture. Add the amount of ice water listed in the recipe to the well, but have more on hand. Use a tossing motion with your hands to start to mix the two together (this begins to combine them without creating too much gluten). As it begins to become hydrated, you can start to use more of a kneading motion, but don't overdo it, as this will make the dough tough. Add more water, about 1 tablespoon (14 grams) at a time, until the dough is properly hydrated. It should be uniformly combined and hold together easily, but it won't look totally smooth. Dough that is too dry may have sort of a "dusty" appearance or pockets of un-hydrated flour. It will not hold together and will appear crumbly. Dough that is too wet will feel sticky or tacky to the touch and is often smoother and/or lighter in color.

4. Form the dough into an even disk (or if you are multiplying the recipe to make multiple crusts, divide the dough appropriately). Wrap tightly in plastic wrap and refrigerate for at least 30 minutes or up to 2 days. (We suggest chilling overnight.)

5. **To Roll Out the Dough:** Lightly dust a work surface with flour, and lightly dust a rolling pin, if desired. Roll out the dough to about ¼ inch thick, rotating it as you work to help prevent it from sticking. To transfer the dough to the pan, gently roll it up, wrapping it around the pin and then unfurl it into the pie plate.

6. **To Prepare the Edge for Crimping:** On a single-crust pie, use scissors to trim away the excess dough, leaving about ½ inch excess all the way around the outside edge of the pie plate. Tuck this excess dough under, pressing gently to make it flush with the edge of the pie plate. On a double-crust pie, gently press the top and bottom crusts together to flatten the dough slightly and then trim the excess and tuck under as directed for a single-crust pie.

7. **To Par-Bake the Dough:** Dock the crimped single-crust pie dough with a fork and chill well (at least 30 minutes). Cut a square of parchment paper slightly larger than the diameter of a pie plate, and press it into the base of the pie plate. Fill with pie weights to the top inner rim of the pie plate. Bake in a 425°F (220°C) oven until the edges begin to lightly brown, 15 to 17 minutes. Remove the parchment paper and pie weights, and return to the oven until the lower portion of the crust appears dry and set, 2 to 3 minutes more. Cool completely before filling.

8. **To Blind-Bake the Dough:** Follow the instructions for par-baking, but bake until it is fully golden brown. After removing the pie weights, bake for 5 to 7 minutes. Cool completely before filling.

Photo by Mark Weinberg

MAKE AHEAD AND STORAGE

The crust can be par-baked up to 1 day ahead. The blueberry filling can be made up to 2 days ahead; refrigerate in an airtight container. The pie can be made up to 1 day ahead; cover pie in plastic wrap, and store in refrigerator. Keep in mind that it's best to add the meringue just before serving. Refrigerate leftovers in an airtight container for up to 2 days.

PASSION FRUIT AND LEMON CURD TART

Makes 1 (9-inch) tart

This tart strikes a satisfying balance between sweet and tart.

4   large eggs (200 grams)
4   large egg yolks (74 grams)
1   cup (200 grams) granulated sugar
¾   cup (180 grams) passion fruit purée*
2   tablespoons (6 grams) lemon zest
¼   cup (60 grams) fresh lemon juice
½   teaspoon (1.5 grams) kosher salt
½   cup (113 grams) unsalted butter, cubed and softened
Pâte Sablée (recipe follows)
Italian Meringue (recipe follows)

1. Place a fine-mesh sieve over a medium bowl; set aside. In another medium bowl, whisk together eggs and egg yolks until well combined; set aside.
2. In a medium saucepan, whisk together sugar, passion fruit purée, lemon zest and juice, and salt. Cook over medium-low heat until sugar is dissolved and mixture begins to steam. (Do not boil.) Pour hot sugar mixture into egg mixture in a slow, steady stream, whisking constantly. Return mixture to saucepan. Cook, stirring slowly and constantly in a figure eight motion with a silicone spatula, until curd is thickened and can coat the back of a spoon and an instant-read thermometer registers 180°F (82°C) and 182°F (83°C), 10 to 12 minutes.
3. Press curd through prepared sieve into bowl, discarding solids. Add butter, 1 to 2 cubes at a time, stirring until melted after each addition. Pour curd into prepared Pâte Sablée. Cover with a piece of plastic wrap, pressing wrap directly onto surface of curd to prevent a skin from forming. Chill until set; refrigerate for at least 4 hours, and freeze for 30 minutes. Alternatively, refrigerate for 24 hours.
4. When ready to serve, top with Italian Meringue. Using a handheld kitchen torch, carefully brown meringue. Serve immediately.

We used Canoa Passion Fruit Purée, available at Latin American food stores or online.

Pâte Sablée
Makes 1 (9-inch) crust

½   cup (113 grams) unsalted butter, softened
⅓   cup (40 grams) confectioners' sugar

1   tablespoon (3 grams) lemon zest
½   teaspoon (1.5 grams) kosher salt
1   large egg yolk (19 grams)
1½   cups (188 grams) pastry flour

1. In the bowl of a stand mixer fitted with the paddle attachment, beat butter at medium speed until smooth, about 1 minute. Add confectioners' sugar, lemon zest, and salt, and beat until smooth, about 1 minute. Add egg yolk, and beat until combined, about 1 minute. Add flour in two additions, beating just until combined.
2. Turn out dough onto a lightly floured surface, and gently knead 3 to 4 times. Shape dough into a disk, and wrap in plastic wrap. Refrigerate for 1 hour.
3. Preheat oven to 325°F (170°C).
4. On a lightly floured surface, roll dough into an 11-inch circle, about ¼ inch thick. Transfer to a 9-inch round tart pan, gently pressing into bottom and completely up sides. Trim excess dough. Freeze until firm, about 10 minutes.
5. Top dough with a piece of parchment paper, letting ends extend over edges of pan. Add pie weights.
6. Bake until edges are light golden brown, about 30 minutes. Carefully remove paper and weights. Bake until crust is golden brown, about 10 minutes more. Let cool completely on a wire rack.

Italian Meringue
Makes 4 cups

1¼   cups (250 grams) granulated sugar
⅓   cup (80 grams) water
½   cup (120 grams) pasteurized egg whites (about 3), room temperature

1. In a small saucepan, heat sugar and ⅓ cup (80 grams) water over high heat until an instant-read thermometer registers 240°F (116°C).
2. Meanwhile, in the bowl of a stand mixer fitted with the whisk attachment, beat egg whites at medium speed until soft peaks form.
3. With mixer running, slowly pour hot sugar syrup into egg whites. Increase mixer speed to high, and beat until bowl is cool to the touch, about 7 minutes. Use immediately.

SWEET POTATO PECAN PIE

Makes 1 (9-inch) pie

A beautiful mash-up of two favorites, this pecan studded sweet potato pie packs the best of both southern desserts into one slice.

Vinegar Pie Dough (recipe follows)

Filling:
2	cups (488 grams) cooked, cubed peeled sweet potato (about 1 pound)
1	cup (200 grams) granulated sugar
¼	cup (57 grams) unsalted butter, melted
¼	cup (60 grams) evaporated milk
3	large eggs (150 grams)
1	teaspoon (1 gram) lemon zest
½	teaspoon (1 gram) pumpkin pie spice
½	teaspoon (2 grams) vanilla extract
¼	teaspoon kosher salt

Egg wash:
1	large egg (50 grams)
1	teaspoon (5 grams) water

Topping:
1½	cups (170 grams) coarsely chopped pecans
⅓	cup (73 grams) firmly packed light brown sugar
2	tablespoons (16 grams) all-purpose flour
2	tablespoons (28 grams) unsalted butter, melted
½	teaspoon (1 gram) pumpkin pie spice
⅛	teaspoon kosher salt

Cane syrup, to serve

1. Preheat oven to 375°F (190°C).
2. Let Vinegar Pie Dough stand at room temperature until slightly softened, about 10 minutes. On a lightly floured surface, roll dough into a 12-inch circle. Transfer to a 9-inch pie plate, pressing into bottom and up sides. Fold edges under, and crimp, if desired. Top with a piece of parchment paper, letting ends extend over edges of plate; add pie weights. Place on a rimmed baking sheet.

3. Bake for 15 minutes. Carefully remove parchment and weights. Let cool on a wire rack for 20 minutes. Reduce oven temperature to 350°F (180°C).
4. For filling: In the work bowl of a food processor, place sweet potato; process until smooth. Transfer sweet potato to a medium bowl. Add granulated sugar, melted butter, evaporated milk, eggs, lemon zest, pie spice, vanilla, and salt, whisking until combined. Pour into prepared crust.
5. For egg wash: In a small bowl, whisk together egg and 1 teaspoon (5 grams) water. Brush egg wash onto crust.
6. Bake in the lower third of the oven until filling is set, about 40 to 50 minutes, covering crust with foil to prevent excess browning, if necessary. Leave oven on.
7. For topping: In a medium bowl, stir together pecans, brown sugar, flour, melted butter, pie spice, and salt with a fork until moistened. Sprinkle topping on pie, leaving a 1-inch border.
8. Bake until pecans are lightly toasted, about 10 minutes, covering crust with foil to prevent excess browning, if necessary. Let cool completely on a wire rack. Drizzle with cane syrup before serving.

VINEGAR PIE DOUGH
Makes 1 (9-inch) crust

1¼	cups (156 grams) all-purpose flour
1	teaspoon (4 grams) granulated sugar
½	teaspoon (1.5 grams) kosher salt
½	cup (113 grams) cold unsalted butter, cubed
5	tablespoons (75 grams) ice water
1	teaspoon (5 grams) distilled white vinegar

1. In a medium bowl, stir together flour, sugar, and salt. Using a pastry blender or 2 forks, cut in cold butter until butter pieces are pea-size.
2. In a small bowl, stir together 5 tablespoons (75 grams) ice water and vinegar. Add vinegar mixture, 1 tablespoon (15 grams) at a time, to flour mixture, stirring until a dough forms. Turn out dough onto a lightly floured surface, and shape into a disk. Wrap tightly in plastic wrap, and refrigerate until firm, at least 1 hour or up to overnight.

PRO TIP
Adding vinegar to pie dough helps keep gluten from forming, ensuring a tender crust.

Makes 1 (9½-inch) tart

A sophisticated twist on buttermilk chess pie, this stunning tart combines a tangy, creamy buttermilk filling with a wine-poached pear topping. Our ginger-scented shortcrust pastry dough and poached pears can be made a day ahead of time, offering a streamlined process for the busy baker.

1   (750-ml) bottle (750 grams) fruity white wine, such as pinot grigio
2½   cups (500 grams) granulated sugar, divided
2   cups (480 grams) water
3   tablespoons (45 grams) fresh lemon juice
2   (2½- to 3-inch) cinnamon sticks
6   whole cloves
2   medium firm ripe Bartlett pears (404 grams), peeled, halved, stemmed, and cored
Ginger Shortcrust Pastry (recipe follows)
2   tablespoons (16 grams) all-purpose flour
¼   teaspoon kosher salt
⅔   cup (160 grams) whole buttermilk, room temperature
⅓   cup (80 grams) heavy whipping cream, room temperature
¼   cup (57 grams) unsalted butter, melted and cooled for 5 minutes
1   large egg (50 grams), room temperature
1   large egg yolk (19 grams), room temperature
2   teaspoons (12 grams) vanilla bean paste
Garnish: finely chopped lightly toasted pistachios, sliced lightly toasted almonds, confectioners' sugar

1. In a large saucepan, combine wine, 2 cups (400 grams) granulated sugar, 2 cups (480 grams) water, lemon juice, cinnamon sticks, and cloves. Bring to a boil over medium-high heat; reduce heat to medium-low, and simmer for 5 minutes. Add pears; place a round of parchment paper on surface of wine mixture, pressing down slightly to help keep pears submerged. Simmer, turning pears occasionally, until pears are fork-tender, 25 to 40 minutes. Using a slotted spoon, transfer pears to a medium heatproof bowl.
2. Discard cinnamon sticks and cloves. Increase heat to medium-high; cook wine mixture until reduced to 3 cups, 15 to 18 minutes. Pour wine mixture over pears in bowl; place a sheet of plastic wrap directly on surface to keep pears submerged, and refrigerate for at least 1 hour.
3. Preheat oven to 350°F (180°C). Spray a 9½-inch fluted round removable-bottom tart pan with baking spray with flour.
4. Let pears in wine mixture stand at room temperature until ready to use.
5. Let Ginger Shortcrust Pastry stand at room temperature until softened, about 15 minutes. On a lightly floured surface, roll dough into a 12-inch circle (about ⅛ inch thick), flouring rolling pin and work surface as needed; trim dough slightly so circle has clean edges. Transfer dough to prepared pan, pressing into bottom and up sides; fold any overhanging dough inside, and press to create a double thickness. (It's OK if dough tears in spots; just press back together.) Using a small sharp knife, trim dough flush with edges of tart pan. Pinch sides lightly so dough sits about ⅛ inch above top edge of pan; use any extra dough to patch thinner spots in crust. Cover and freeze for 15 minutes.

POACHED PEAR BUTTERMILK PIE

6. Place tart pan on a parchment-lined rimmed baking sheet. Top frozen dough with a sheet of parchment paper, letting ends extend over edges of tart pan. Add pie weights.
7. Bake until edges are lightly golden, 15 to 20 minutes, rotating pan halfway through baking. Carefully remove parchment and weights. Bake until crust is dry and set, about 5 minutes more. Let cool completely on baking sheet on a wire rack. Leave oven on.
8. In the bowl of a stand mixer, whisk together flour, salt, and remaining ½ cup (100 grams) granulated sugar by hand. Add buttermilk, cream, melted butter, egg, egg yolk, and vanilla bean paste; using the whisk attachment, beat at medium speed until smooth and well combined, stopping to scrape sides of bowl.
9. Using a slotted spoon, remove pear halves from wine mixture. Pat pears dry, and slice each half lengthwise into 8 wedges. Arrange wedges in a tight overlapping circular pattern along edge of prepared crust. Pour buttermilk mixture in center of crust, shaking pan gently to evenly distribute between pears. (Pan will be quite full but will not overflow during baking.)
10. Bake until filling is just set (it may still jiggle in center) and an instant-read thermometer inserted in center registers 170°F (76°C) to 175°F (79°C), 25 to 28 minutes. Let cool completely on baking sheet on a wire rack. Remove from tart pan. Before serving, garnish with pistachios, almonds, and confectioners' sugar, if desired.

GINGER SHORTCRUST PASTRY
Makes 1 (9½-inch) crust

1¾   cups (219 grams) all-purpose flour
⅓   cup (67 grams) granulated sugar
1½   teaspoons (3 grams) ground ginger
½   teaspoon (1.5 grams) kosher salt
½   cup (113 grams) cold unsalted butter, cubed
1   large egg (50 grams), lightly beaten

1. In the work bowl of a food processor, place flour, sugar, ginger, and salt; pulse until combined. Add cold butter, and pulse until mixture resembles coarse crumbs. Add egg, and pulse just until dough comes together, stopping to scrape sides of bowl. (Mixture should be moist but not sticky and should hold together when pinched.)
2. Turn out dough, and shape into a 7-inch disk. Wrap in plastic wrap, and refrigerate for at least 25 minutes.

SWEET POTATO TART

Makes 1 (9½-inch) tart

A twist on the classic sweet potato pie, our tart has a speculoos cookie crust filled with vanilla bean seed-speckled sweet potato filling and garnished with a billowy meringue that'll inspire only the fluffiest of marshmallow fantasies.

1⅓ cups (202 grams) firmly packed finely crushed speculaas cookies* (about 26 cookies)
¼ cup (57 grams) unsalted butter, melted
1¼ teaspoons (2.5 grams) ground cinnamon, divided
½ teaspoon kosher salt, divided
5 ounces (142 grams) cream cheese, room temperature
1¼ cups (295 grams) puréed cooked peeled sweet potato (see Note)
½ cup (110 grams) firmly packed light brown sugar
2 teaspoons (6 grams) all-purpose flour
¾ teaspoon (4.5 grams) vanilla bean paste
½ teaspoon (1 gram) ground ginger
⅛ teaspoon ground cloves
2 large eggs (100 grams), room temperature
Vanilla Bean Meringue (recipe follows)

1. Preheat oven to 350°F (180°C). Spray a 9½-inch fluted round removable-bottom tart pan with baking spray with flour.
2. In a large bowl, stir together crushed cookies, melted butter, ½ teaspoon (1 gram) cinnamon, and ¼ teaspoon salt until well combined; using a small straight-sided measuring cup, press mixture into bottom and up sides of prepared pan.
3. Bake until set and fragrant, 8 to 10 minutes. Let cool completely on a wire rack. Reduce oven temperature to 325°F (170°C).
4. In the bowl of a stand mixer fitted with the paddle attachment, beat cream cheese at medium speed until smooth and creamy, about 2 minutes, stopping to scrape sides of bowl. Add sweet potato, brown sugar, flour, vanilla bean paste, ginger, cloves, remaining ¾ teaspoon (1.5 grams) cinnamon, and remaining ¼ teaspoon salt; beat at medium-low speed just until combined. Increase mixer speed to medium, and beat until well combined, about 2 minutes, stopping to scrape sides of bowl. Add eggs, one at a time, beating until well combined after each addition and stopping to scrape sides of bowl. (Mixture will be on the thicker side.) Spoon into prepared crust; using a small offset spatula, spread into an even layer.

5. Bake until top is set and an instant-read thermometer inserted in center registers 155°F (68°C), 22 to 28 minutes. Let cool completely in pan on a wire rack; cover and refrigerate for at least 8 hours or overnight.
6. Carefully remove tart from pan; transfer to a serving plate. Spoon and spread Vanilla Bean Meringue onto tart as desired. Using a handheld kitchen torch, carefully brown meringue as desired. Serve immediately.

We used Biscoff Cookies.

Note: *We liked the bright color and convenience of using pre-cubed raw sweet potatoes, sold in 1-pound bags in the produce department and designed to be steamed right in their package. Cook according to package directions, then puree in a food processor until mostly smooth.*

Vanilla Bean Meringue
Makes about 5 cups

1¼ cups (250 grams) granulated sugar
6 large egg whites (180 grams), room temperature
¼ teaspoon (1 gram) cream of tartar
¼ teaspoon kosher salt
2 teaspoons (12 grams) vanilla bean paste

1. In the heatproof bowl of a stand mixer, whisk together sugar, egg whites, cream of tartar, and salt. Place over a saucepan of simmering water, and cook, stirring frequently, until an instant-read thermometer registers 160°F (71°C), 15 to 20 minutes.
2. Return bowl to stand mixer. Using the whisk attachment, beat sugar mixture at medium-high speed until bowl is room temperature and meringue forms glossy stiff peaks, about 10 minutes. Beat in vanilla bean paste. Use immediately.

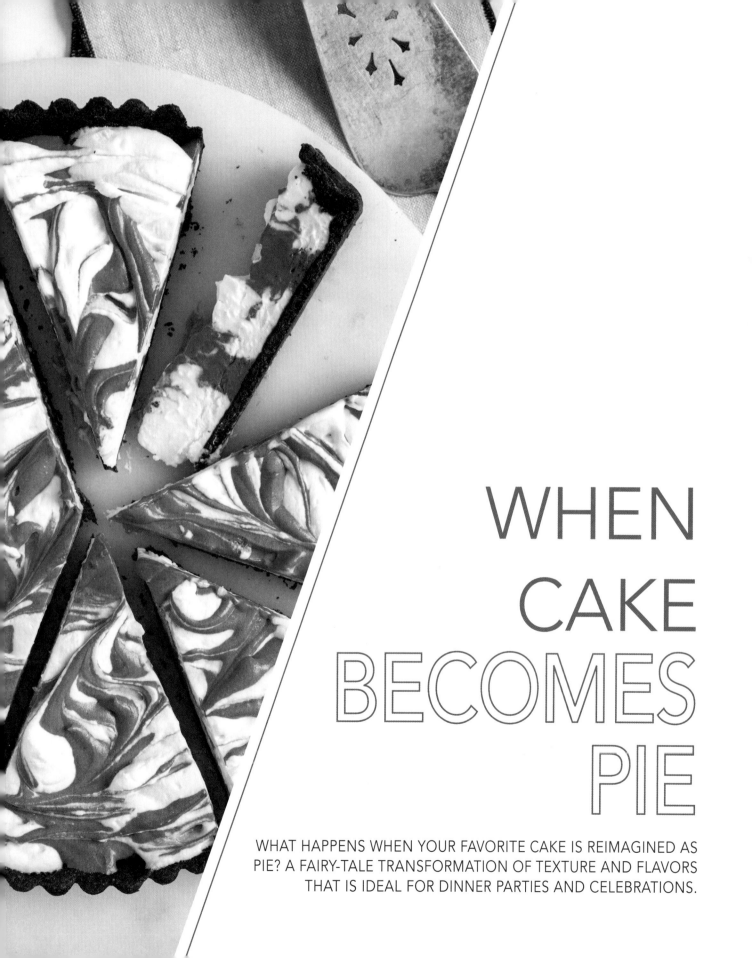

WHEN CAKE BECOMES PIE

WHAT HAPPENS WHEN YOUR FAVORITE CAKE IS REIMAGINED AS PIE? A FAIRY-TALE TRANSFORMATION OF TEXTURE AND FLAVORS THAT IS IDEAL FOR DINNER PARTIES AND CELEBRATIONS.

BLACK FOREST PIE

Makes 1 (9-inch) pie

The secret to this dessert is Kirsch liqueur (also known as kirschwasser), a unique cherry spirit that uses the flavoring from both cherries and their stones, imparting a delicious almond aftertaste.

1¼   cups (156 grams) all-purpose flour
3   tablespoons (15 grams) Dutch process cocoa powder
2   teaspoons (6 grams) kosher salt
1½   teaspoons (6 grams) granulated sugar
½   cup (113 grams) cold unsalted butter, cubed
6   tablespoons (90 grams) ice water
Bittersweet Cherry Ganache (recipe follows)
Cherry Mousse (recipe follows)
Garnish: fresh cherries

1. In the work bowl of a food processor, place flour, cocoa, salt, and sugar; pulse until combined. Add cold butter, pulsing until mixture is crumbly. With processor running, add ice water, 1 tablespoon (15 grams) at a time, just until a dough forms. Turn out dough, and shape into a disk. Wrap tightly in plastic wrap, and refrigerate for at least 30 minutes.
2. Let dough stand at room temperature until slightly softened, about 5 minutes. On a lightly floured surface, roll dough into a 12-inch circle. Transfer to a 9-inch pie plate, pressing into bottom and up sides. Trim excess dough to ½ inch beyond edge of plate. Fold edges under, and crimp, if desired. Prick bottom of dough with a fork. Refrigerate for 30 minutes.
3. Preheat oven to 350°F (180°C).
4. Top dough with a piece of parchment paper, letting ends extend over edges of plate. Add pie weights.
5. Bake for 15 minutes. Carefully remove paper and weights. Bake 10 minutes more. Let cool completely on a wire rack.
6. Spoon Bittersweet Cherry Ganache into prepared crust, smoothing with an offset spatula. Refrigerate until set, about 15 minutes. Pour Cherry Mousse over ganache, and refrigerate until set, about 45 minutes. Garnish with cherries, if desired.

BITTERSWEET CHERRY GANACHE
Makes about ¾ cup

7   ounces (200 grams) 60% cacao bittersweet chocolate, chopped
1   tablespoon (15 grams) kirschwasser cherry liqueur
¼   cup (60 grams) heavy whipping cream
¼   cup (60 grams) cherry purée (see PRO TIP)

1. In a medium bowl, combine chocolate and cherry liqueur.
2. In a small saucepan, bring cream and cherry purée to a boil over medium heat. Pour hot cream mixture over chocolate mixture, and whisk until smooth and shiny. Use immediately.

CHERRY MOUSSE
Makes about 2½ cups

1⅓   cups (320 grams) heavy whipping cream, divided
⅓   cup (80 grams) plus 3 tablespoons (45 grams) cold whole milk, divided
5   large egg yolks (93 grams)
3   tablespoons (36 grams) granulated sugar
2   tablespoons (16 grams) cornstarch
2   teaspoons (8 grams) unflavored gelatin
⅓   cup plus 1 tablespoon (95 grams) cherry purée (see PRO TIP)
6   ounces (175 grams) white chocolate morsels
2   tablespoons (30 grams) kirschwasser cherry liqueur

1. In a medium saucepan, bring ⅔ cup (160 grams) cream and ⅓ cup (80 grams) milk to a boil over medium heat.
2. In a medium bowl, whisk together egg yolks, sugar, cornstarch, gelatin, and remaining 3 tablespoons (45 grams) cold milk. Whisking constantly, slowly pour hot cream mixture into yolk mixture. Return cream mixture to saucepan, and cook, whisking constantly, until mixture has thickened, about 1 minute.
3. In another medium bowl, combine cherry purée, chocolate morsels, and cherry liqueur. Strain cream mixture over cherry mixture, and whisk until smooth. Place bowl in a larger bowl filled with ice. Let cool to room temperature over ice bath, whisking constantly to ensure even cooling and to prevent mousse from creating lumps. (If mousse cools any further than room temperature, it will become too thick.)
4. In the bowl of a stand mixer fitted with the whisk attachment, beat remaining ⅔ cup (160 grams) cream at high speed until soft peaks form. Fold whipped cream into mousse until smooth.

PRO TIP
To make **cherry purée**, place 1 pound (455 grams) fresh pitted cherries in the work bowl of a food processor. Purée until smooth. Strain mixture, discarding solids. This will yield about 1 cup cherry purée.

PLUM-AND-PRETZEL CHEESECAKE PIE

Makes 1 (9-inch) pie

Recipe by Marian Cooper Cairns

Salty pretzels are an excellent base for this slightly sweet mascarpone cheesecake. The plums macerate in a mixture of brown sugar and nutmeg and then bake directly on the cheesecake batter. Finish this dessert with an orange-scented glaze for a pretty presentation.

4   large plums (360 grams), pitted and cut into ¼-inch-thick slices
6   tablespoons (84 grams) firmly packed light brown sugar, divided
½   teaspoon (1.5 grams) kosher salt
¼   teaspoon ground nutmeg
2   cups (186 grams) finely ground pretzels
10 tablespoons (140 grams) unsalted butter, melted
¼   cup (50 grams) granulated sugar
8   ounces (225 grams) mascarpone cheese, softened
4   ounces (115 grams) cream cheese, softened
1   large egg (50 grams)
2   teaspoons (8 grams) vanilla extract
1   teaspoon (2 grams) orange zest
1   tablespoon (15 grams) orange liqueur*
½   teaspoon (1.5 grams) cornstarch

1. In a large bowl, toss together plums, 4 tablespoons (56 grams) brown sugar, salt, and nutmeg. Let stand for 45 minutes, stirring every 15 minutes.
2. Preheat oven to 350°F (180°C).
3. In a large bowl, stir together pretzels, melted butter, and granulated sugar until combined. Press pretzel mixture firmly into a 9-inch pie plate.
4. Bake until golden around the edges, 10 to 12 minutes. Let cool completely. Reduce oven temperature to 325°F (170°C).

5. In the bowl of a stand mixer fitted with the paddle attachment, beat mascarpone, cream cheese, and remaining 2 tablespoons (28 grams) brown sugar at medium speed until smooth. Add egg, vanilla, and zest, beating until combined. Spoon into prepared crust.
6. Drain plums, reserving ¼ cup (60 grams) juice. Arrange plums on top of mascarpone mixture in a circular pattern, slightly overlapping (you may have a few leftover plum slices).
7. Bake until filling is set, 45 to 55 minutes. Let cool completely on a wire rack.
8. In a small saucepan, whisk together reserved ¼ cup (60 grams) plum juice, orange liqueur, and cornstarch. Bring to a boil over medium heat, and cook until thickened. Brush over pie. Refrigerate for at least 3 hours or overnight.

We used Grand Marnier.

Photo by Matt Armendariz

STRAWBERRY SWIRL CHEESECAKE PIE

Makes 1 (9-inch) pie

For a hint of subtle heat, we added a pinch of black pepper to the crust of this rich cheesecake pie.

1½   cups (195 grams) graham cracker crumbs
7   tablespoons (98 grams) unsalted butter, melted
⅔   cup (133 grams) plus 2 tablespoons (24 grams) granulated sugar, divided
½   teaspoon (1 gram) ground black pepper
¼   teaspoon kosher salt
16   ounces (450 grams) cream cheese, softened
1   tablespoon (8 grams) all-purpose flour
2   large eggs (100 grams)
¼   cup (60 grams) sour cream, room temperature
1   teaspoon (4 grams) vanilla extract
⅔   cup (213 grams) strawberry preserves
½   cup (85 grams) chopped fresh strawberries

1. Preheat oven to 350°F (180°C). Butter and flour a 9-inch pie plate.
2. In a medium bowl, stir together graham cracker crumbs, melted butter, 2 tablespoons (24 grams) sugar, pepper, and salt. Using a measuring cup, press mixture into bottom and up sides of prepared plate.
3. Bake for 5 minutes. Let cool on a wire rack. Reduce oven temperature to 325°F (170°C).
4. In the bowl of a stand mixer fitted with the paddle attachment, beat cream cheese at medium speed until creamy, stopping to scrape sides of bowl. Add flour and remaining ⅔ cup (133 grams) sugar, beating until combined. Add eggs, one at a time, beating just until combined after each addition (do not overbeat). Reduce mixer speed to low. Add sour cream and vanilla, beating until smooth. Pour into prepared crust.
5. In the container of a blender, place preserves and strawberries; blend until smooth. Drizzle 5 tablespoons (100 grams) strawberry mixture over filling. Using the tip of a knife, gently swirl over top of pie. Refrigerate remaining strawberry mixture.
6. Bake until edges are set and slightly puffed, 35 to 45 minutes. Let cool on a wire rack for 1 hour. Refrigerate until cold, about 3 hours. Serve with remaining strawberry mixture.

HUMMINGBIRD PIE

Makes 1 (9-inch) pie

In this twist on the classic cake, billowy peaks of homemade Buttermilk Whipped Cream blanket a silky yellow custard.

1 cup (240 grams) coconut milk, room temperature
1 cup (240 grams) pineapple juice
4 large egg yolks (74 grams), room temperature
1 large egg (50 grams), room temperature
½ cup (100 grams) granulated sugar
3 tablespoons (24 grams) cornstarch
½ teaspoon (1.5 grams) kosher salt
2 tablespoons (28 grams) unsalted butter, cubed
2 tablespoons (30 grams) light rum
3 medium bananas (282 grams), sliced ¼ inch thick
Pecan Piecrust (recipe follows)
Buttermilk Whipped Cream (recipe follows)

1. In a medium saucepan, heat coconut milk and pineapple juice over medium heat, stirring frequently, just until bubbles form around edges of pan. (Do not boil.) Remove from heat.
2. In a medium bowl, whisk together egg yolks, egg, sugar, cornstarch, and salt. Gradually add hot milk mixture to egg mixture, whisking constantly. Return mixture to saucepan, and cook, whisking constantly, until thickened. Pour through a fine-mesh sieve into a medium bowl, discarding solids. Stir in butter and rum until butter is melted. Cover with a piece of plastic wrap, pressing wrap directly onto surface of cream to prevent a skin from forming. Refrigerate overnight.
3. Place banana slices in two even layers in bottom of prepared Pecan Piecrust. Pour pineapple-coconut cream over banana slices, smoothing top with an offset spatula. Refrigerate for 1 to 2 hours. Top with Buttermilk Whipped Cream before serving.

Pecan Piecrust
Makes 1 (9-inch) crust

1½ cups (188 grams) all-purpose flour
½ cup (57 grams) pecan halves
1½ teaspoons (6 grams) granulated sugar
1 teaspoon (2 grams) ground cinnamon
½ teaspoon (1.5 grams) kosher salt
½ teaspoon (1 gram) ground nutmeg
½ cup (113 grams) cold unsalted butter, cubed
¼ cup (60 grams) ice water

1. In the work bowl of a food processor, place flour, pecans, sugar, cinnamon, salt, and nutmeg; process until combined. Add cold butter, and pulse until mixture is crumbly. With processor running, add ¼ cup (60 grams) ice water in a slow, steady stream just until dough comes together. (Mixture may appear crumbly. It should be moist and hold together when pinched.) Shape dough into a disk, and wrap tightly in plastic wrap. Refrigerate for at least 30 minutes.
2. On a lightly floured surface, roll dough into a 12-inch circle. Transfer to a 9-inch pie plate, pressing into bottom and up sides. Trim excess dough to ½ inch beyond edge of plate. Fold edges under, and crimp as desired. Using a fork, prick bottom of crust. Freeze for 20 minutes.
3. Preheat oven to 350°F (180°C).
4. Top dough with a piece of parchment paper, letting ends extend over edges of plate. Add pie weights.
5. Bake until edges are set and golden, 15 to 20 minutes. Carefully remove paper and weights. Bake until bottom of crust is lightly golden, about 10 minutes more. Let cool completely.

Buttermilk Whipped Cream
Makes about 1½ cups

1 cup (240 grams) heavy whipping cream, room temperature
½ cup (120 grams) whole buttermilk, room temperature
2 tablespoons (24 grams) granulated sugar
¼ teaspoon kosher salt

1. In the bowl of a stand mixer fitted with the whisk attachment, beat all ingredients at medium-high speed until stiff peaks form, 2 to 3 minutes. Use immediately.

Photo by Stephen DeVries

BOURBON-PINEAPPLE POUND TART

Makes 1 (10-inch) tart

Recipe by Ben Mims

Pound cakes have long been relegated to large, deep pans, and for good reason: The heaviness of the cakes means they don't rise much and need to "settle" into pans that already have structure in order to bake up well. But for this cake, Ben went with a large, deep tart pan to produce a sleek, slim wedge of cake that eats like a tart, complete with fluted edge and chunks of fresh fruit on top.

¾   cup (170 grams) unsalted butter, softened
1½   cups (300 grams) granulated sugar
2   tablespoons plus 1 teaspoon (35 grams) bourbon, divided
1   teaspoon (3 grams) kosher salt
1   teaspoon (4 grams) vanilla extract
½   teaspoon (2.5 grams) baking powder
3   large eggs (150 grams), room temperature
1½   cups (187 grams) cake flour
8   ounces (225 grams) peeled and cored fresh pineapple, cut into ½-inch chunks
2   cups (240 grams) confectioners' sugar
2   tablespoons (28 grams) fresh pineapple juice
1   ring candied pineapple

1. Preheat oven to 325°F (170°C). Butter and flour a tall-sided 10-inch removable-bottom fluted tart pan.

2. In the bowl of a stand mixer fitted with the paddle attachment, beat butter, granulated sugar, 1 tablespoon (15 grams) bourbon, salt, vanilla, and baking powder at medium speed until fluffy and pale, at least 6 minutes. Add eggs, one at a time, beating until there are no streaks of yolk left after each addition, about 15 seconds. Scrape bottom and sides of bowl with a rubber spatula. With mixer on medium-high speed, beat until superlight and airy, at least 3 minutes. Add flour, and stir with a rubber spatula just until combined. Spoon batter into prepared pan, and smooth top.

3. Place pineapple chunks on a layer of paper towels to dry thoroughly; scatter pineapple over batter.

4. Bake until golden brown and a wooden pick inserted in center comes out clean, 1 hour and 15 minutes to 1 hour and 30 minutes. Let cool in pan for 30 minutes. Carefully loosen edges of pan from tart. Lift bottom of pan to unmold it from outer ring. Loosen bottom of pan from tart, and slide tart onto a wire rack.

5. In a medium bowl, whisk together confectioners' sugar, pineapple juice, and remaining 1 tablespoon plus 1 teaspoon (20 grams) bourbon.

6. Using a fork, drizzle pineapple glaze back and forth over top of tart, letting it fall over sides. Thinly slice candied pineapple ring into matchsticks, and sprinkle over top of tart while glaze is still wet. Let stand for at least 10 minutes to let icing set before serving.

RASPBERRY LEMON CHIFFON PIE

Makes 1 (9-inch) pie

Much like the lighter-than-air chiffon cake this pie is inspired by, the dreamy raspberry filling receives a soft and fluffy texture boost from whipped egg whites. A buttery speculaas cookie crust balances out the berry citrus filling while a toasty Lemon Swiss Meringue topping adds a touch of marshmallow-like decadence.

1½   cups (180 grams) crushed speculaas cookies*
¼   cup (50 grams) granulated sugar
¼   cup (57 grams) unsalted butter, melted
¼   teaspoon kosher salt
Raspberry Lemon Filling (recipe follows)
Lemon Swiss Meringue (recipe follows)
Garnish: fresh raspberries, grated lemon zest

1. Preheat oven to 350°F (180°C).
2. In a medium bowl, stir together crushed cookies, sugar, melted butter, and salt. Press mixture into bottom and up sides of 9-inch pie plate.
3. Bake for 10 minutes. Pour Raspberry Lemon Filling into prepared crust. Top with Lemon Swiss Meringue. Using a kitchen torch, brown meringue. Garnish with raspberries and zest, if desired.

RASPBERRY LEMON FILLING

Makes about 1½ cups

1½   cups (255 grams) fresh raspberries, divided
¼   cup (50 grams) plus 1 tablespoon (12 grams) granulated sugar, divided
¼   cup (60 grams) water
2   tablespoons (6 grams) lemon zest
1   tablespoon (15 grams) fresh lemon juice
½   teaspoon (1.5 grams) kosher salt
2   tablespoons (18 grams) tapioca flour
1   tablespoon (12 grams) unflavored gelatin
4   large egg whites (120 grams)

1. In a small saucepan, bring ½ cup (85 grams) raspberries, ¼ cup (50 grams) sugar, ¼ cup (60 grams) water, lemon zest and juice, and salt to a boil over medium heat. Whisk in flour and gelatin; cook until thickened, 2 to 3 minutes. Let cool to room temperature.
2. In the bowl of a stand mixer fitted with the whisk attachment, beat egg whites and remaining 1 tablespoon (12 grams) sugar at high speed until soft peaks form. Fold into raspberry mixture. Fold in remaining 1 cup (170 grams) raspberries.

*We used Biscoff Cookies.

LEMON SWISS MERINGUE

Makes about 2 cups

1   cup (200 grams) granulated sugar
4   large egg whites (120 grams)
1   tablespoon (3 grams) lemon zest

1. In the top of a double boiler, whisk together all ingredients. Cook over simmering water, stirring constantly, until sugar is dissolved and a candy thermometer registers 140°F (60°C). Transfer to the bowl of a stand mixer fitted with the whisk attachment. Beat at high speed until stiff and glossy peaks form, 8 to 10 minutes.

FROZEN GERMAN CHOCOLATE TART

Makes 1 (10-inch) tart

What happens when a coconut-and-chocolate-laden classic becomes a tart? Magic in the making. Toasted pecans and flaked coconut are studded throughout a lightened dulce de leche no-bake filling, while melted chocolate gives this rendition its characteristic richness.

Vanilla Shortcrust (recipe follows)
2   (13.4-ounce) cans (746 grams) dulce de leche
1½ cups (126 grams) sweetened flaked coconut, toasted
1   cup (113 grams) finely chopped toasted pecans
1¾ teaspoons (5.25 grams) kosher salt, divided
1   teaspoon (6 grams) vanilla bean paste, divided
1¼ cups (300 grams) cold heavy whipping cream
1   (8-ounce) package (226 grams) cream cheese, cubed and room temperature
1   (14-ounce) can (380 grams) sweetened condensed milk
8   ounces (226 grams) 70% cacao bittersweet chocolate baking bars, melted (see Notes)
Garnish: finely chopped toasted pecans, toasted sweetened flaked coconut

1. Let Vanilla Shortcrust stand at room temperature until slightly softened, 10 to 15 minutes. (See Notes.)
2. Spray a tall-sided 10-inch fluted round removable-bottom tart pan with baking spray with flour.
3. On a lightly floured surface, roll Vanilla Shortcrust into a 14-inch circle (about ⅛ to ¼ inch thick), flouring rolling pin and work surface as needed. Gently transfer dough to prepared pan, pressing into bottom and up sides. (It's OK if dough tears in spots; press back together using a fingertip dipped in water to thoroughly seal any seams.) Using a small sharp knife, trim dough flush with sides of pan; pinch sides lightly so dough sits about ⅛- to 1/16-inch above top edge of pan, and use any excess dough to patch thinner spots in crust. Freeze until firm, 15 to 25 minutes.
4. Preheat oven to 350°F (180°C).
5. Place tart pan on a rimmed baking sheet. Top with parchment paper, letting ends extend over edges of pan; add pie weights.
6. Bake until edges are dry, just set, and lightly golden, 18 to 22 minutes, rotating pan halfway through baking. Carefully remove parchment and weights. Using the tines of a fork, dock bottom of crust. Bake until inside and bottom of crust is lightly golden, dry,

and set, 20 to 27 minutes, lightly covering edges with foil to prevent excess browning, if necessary. (It's OK if crust shrinks slightly; if bottom puffs, gently push down with a heatproof spoon.) Let cool completely in pan on a wire rack.
7. In a large bowl, stir together dulce de leche, coconut, pecans, 1 teaspoon (3 grams) salt, and ½ teaspoon (3 grams) vanilla bean paste until well combined. Set aside.
8. In the bowl of a stand mixer fitted with the whisk attachment, beat cold cream at medium-high speed until medium-stiff peaks form. Transfer to a medium bowl.
9. Clean bowl of stand mixer and whisk attachment. Using the whisk attachment, beat cream cheese at medium speed until smooth and creamy, 1 to 2 minutes, stopping to scrape sides of bowl. Add condensed milk, melted chocolate, remaining ¾ teaspoon (2.25 grams) salt, and remaining ½ teaspoon (3 grams) vanilla bean paste; beat until well combined, stopping to scrape sides of bowl. Fold in whipped cream in three additions. Place 1½ cups (273 grams) cream cheese mixture in a pastry bag fitted with a medium open star piping tip (Wilton No. 1M); set aside. Spoon half of remaining cream cheese mixture into cooled prepared crust, smoothing top with a small offset spatula. Freeze for 15 minutes.
10. Place half of dulce de leche mixture into another large pastry bag; cut a ¾-inch opening in tip. Pipe dulce de leche mixture evenly over cream cheese mixture in crust, gently smoothing with a small offset spatula. Top with remaining cream cheese mixture, smoothing with a small offset spatula. Freeze for 15 minutes.
11. Spoon remaining dulce de leche mixture into pastry bag; pipe on top of cream cheese mixture, leaving a ½- to ¾-inch border, piling high and smoothing or texturing with a small offset spatula, as necessary.
12. Pipe reserved cream cheese mixture around edge of tart; garnish with pecans and coconut, if desired. Freeze until firm, at least 4 hours. (Alternatively, refrigerate overnight.) Let stand at room temperature for 30 minutes to 1 hour. Remove from pan, and serve.

Notes: *To melt our chocolate, we used the double boiler method. In the top of a double boiler, place chopped chocolate. (Do not attempt to melt chocolate bars whole.) Cook over simmering water, stirring frequently, until melted and smooth.*

Dough refrigerated overnight may need to stand at room temperature until slightly softened, 30 to 45 minutes, before rolling.

PRO TIP
If desired, use a kitchen torch to gently warm sides of pan to release tart. Let tart stand at room temperature for 30 minutes to 1 hour before serving.

Vanilla Shortcrust

Makes 1 (10-inch) crust

1   cup (227 grams) cold unsalted butter
2⅔   cups (333 grams) all-purpose flour
2   tablespoons (24 grams) granulated sugar
2   teaspoons (6 grams) kosher salt
3   tablespoons (45 grams) cold whole milk
2   large egg yolks (37 grams)
1   teaspoon (6 grams) vanilla bean paste

1. Cut butter into ½- to ¾-inch cubes. Freeze until firm, about 10 minutes.

2. In the bowl of a stand mixer, whisk together flour, sugar, and salt by hand. Add frozen butter; using the paddle attachment, beat at low speed until butter is broken into small pieces, 2 to 3 minutes. (If any large pieces of butter remain, squeeze between fingers to break up.)

3. In a 1-cup liquid-measuring cup, whisk together milk, egg yolks, and vanilla bean paste. With mixer on very low speed, add milk mixture to flour mixture in a slow, steady stream, beating just until moist clumps form. Transfer mixture to a large piece of plastic wrap. Using your hands, bring mixture together to form a cohesive dough. Shape dough into a 7-inch disk, and wrap in plastic wrap. Refrigerate for at least 1 hour or up to overnight.

MINT CHIP PIE

Makes 1 (9-inch) pie

You're not dreaming—this spectacular treat was inspired by your favorite grasshopper cake. With dark chocolate studded throughout its irresistible green interior, this pie is almost too pretty to eat. Almost.

Black Cocoa Pie Dough (recipe follows)
1½ cups (360 grams) cold heavy whipping cream
12 ounces (340 grams) cream cheese, softened
1½ cups (180 grams) confectioners' sugar
¼ teaspoon kosher salt
½ teaspoon (2 grams) peppermint extract
Green gel food coloring*
⅓ cup (57 grams) finely chopped 70% cacao dark chocolate
Sweetened Whipped Cream (recipe follows)
Garnish: chocolate shavings

1. Preheat oven to 400°F (200°C).
2. On a lightly floured surface, roll Black Cocoa Pie Dough into a 12-inch circle. Gently transfer to a 9-inch pie plate, pressing into bottom and up sides. Trim dough even with edge of plate, if necessary. Freeze until firm, about 30 minutes.
3. Top Black Cocoa Pie Dough with a piece of parchment paper, letting ends extend over edges of plate. Add pie weights.
4. Bake until edges look dry, 15 to 20 minutes. Carefully remove parchment and weights. Bake until crust is completely dry, 5 to 7 minutes more. Let cool completely on a wire rack.
5. In the bowl of a stand mixer fitted with the whisk attachment, beat cold cream at medium-high speed until soft peaks form. Transfer to medium bowl.
6. Clean bowl of stand mixer. Using the paddle attachment, beat cream cheese at medium speed until smooth, about 2 minutes. Add confectioners' sugar and salt, and beat at low speed until smooth, about 4 minutes, stopping to scrape sides of bowl halfway through mixing. Using a spatula, gently fold in whipped cream just until combined. Fold in peppermint extract and green food coloring as desired. Fold in chopped chocolate. Pour into cooled prepared crust, and using a small offset spatula, smooth top. Refrigerate until filling is set, 5 to 6 hours.
7. Place Sweetened Whipped Cream in a large pastry bag fitted with large St. Honoré piping tip (Wilton No. 125). On outside edge of filling, pipe a 1½-inch diagonal line going toward center. Starting at the halfway point of piped line, pipe another 1½-inch diagonal line in opposite direction, slight overlapping end of previous line. (It will look like an offset "V.") Repeat pattern around edges. Refrigerate until ready to serve. Garnish with chocolate shavings, if desired.

We used Wilton Icing Color in Leaf Green.

BLACK COCOA PIE DOUGH
Makes 1 (9-inch) crust

1½ cups (188 grams) all-purpose flour
¼ cup (50 grams) granulated sugar
¼ cup (21 grams) black cocoa powder
1 teaspoon (3 grams) kosher salt
⅔ cup (150 grams) cold unsalted butter, cut into small cubes
1 large egg (50 grams)

1. In the work bowl of a food processor, place flour, sugar, black cocoa, and salt; pulse until combined. Add cold butter and egg, pulsing just until combined and mixture holds together when pressed, 24 to 30 pulses. Turn out dough onto a lightly floured surface, and shape into a disk. Wrap in plastic wrap, and refrigerate for at least 1 hour.

SWEETENED WHIPPED CREAM
Makes about 2 cups

1 cup (240 grams) cold heavy whipping cream
¼ cup (50 grams) granulated sugar

1. In the bowl of a stand mixer fitted with the whisk attachment, beat cream and sugar at medium-high speed until medium-soft peaks form, about 3 to 5 minutes. Use immediately, or refrigerate until ready to use. Best used same day.

BIRTHDAY "PIE"

Makes 8 to 10 servings

With vibrant color and crave-worthy crunch, rainbow sprinkles simply add extra joy to a celebration. If you are looking to satisfy a pie enthusiast on their birthday or searching for a way to switch up your usual cake, this Birthday Pie is the ultimate party treat.

¾	cup (170 grams) unsalted butter, softened
¾	cup (150 grams) granulated sugar
⅓	cup (73 grams) firmly packed light brown sugar
1	large egg (50 grams), room temperature
1	large egg yolk (19 grams), room temperature
1½	teaspoons (6 grams) vanilla extract
½	teaspoon (2 grams) almond extract
1½	cups (188 grams) unbleached cake flour
1	teaspoon (3 grams) kosher salt
¼	teaspoon (1.25 grams) baking powder
⅓	cup (80 grams) whole buttermilk, room temperature
⅓	cup (64 grams) plus 1 tablespoon (10 grams) rainbow sprinkles*, divided

Vanilla-Almond Buttercream (recipe follows)

1. Preheat oven to 325°F (170°C).
2. In the bowl of a stand mixer fitted with the paddle attachment, beat butter and sugars at medium-low speed just until combined. Increase mixer speed to medium; beat until fluffy, 3 to 4 minutes, stopping to scrape sides of bowl. Add egg and egg yolk, one at a time, beating well after each addition. Beat in extracts.
3. In a large bowl, whisk together flour, salt, and baking powder. With mixer on low speed, gradually add flour mixture to butter mixture alternately with buttermilk, beginning and ending with flour mixture, beating just until combined after each addition. Gently fold in ⅓ cup (64 grams) sprinkles.
4. Spray a tall-sided 10-inch fluted round removable-bottom tart pan with baking spray with flour. Spoon batter into prepared pan, smoothing top with a small offset spatula. Sprinkle remaining 1 tablespoon (10 grams) sprinkles on top.

5. Bake until a wooden pick inserted in center comes out clean, 30 to 35 minutes. Let cool in pan for 10 minutes. Carefully remove sides of pan; let cool completely on pan base on a wire rack.
6. Using a large offset spatula, carefully loosen cake from pan base; place cake on a serving plate. Spoon Vanilla-Almond Buttercream into a pastry bag fitted with a coupler; pipe buttercream on top of cooled cake using assorted small piping tips (Wilton No. 10, Wilton No. 21, Wilton No. 199). Garnish with sprinkles, if desired.

We used Betty Crocker Rainbow Jimmies.

Vanilla-Almond Buttercream
Makes about 1¼ cups

6	tablespoons (84 grams) unsalted butter, softened
¼	teaspoon kosher salt
1½	cups (180 grams) confectioners' sugar
1½	tablespoons (22.5 grams) heavy whipping cream
¼	teaspoon (1 gram) vanilla extract
¼	teaspoon (1 gram) almond extract

1. In the bowl of a stand mixer fitted with the paddle attachment, beat butter and salt at medium speed until creamy, about 1 minute, stopping to scrape sides of bowl.
2. With mixer on low speed, gradually add confectioners' sugar alternately with cream, beginning and ending with confectioners' sugar, beating just until combined. Beat in extracts.
3. Increase mixer speed to medium; beat until light and fluffy, 2 to 3 minutes, stopping to scrape sides of bowl. Use immediately.

CHERRY BASQUE TART

Makes 1 (9-inch) pie

It's no secret that I am a gateaux Basque fanatic. Ever since I first tasted the creamy interior enveloped by the flaky buttery crust, it was love at first bite. From Bundts to cookies—and now to pie—if I can "Basque-it" and share these flavors with the world, it's all fair game.

Pâte Sablé Crust (recipe follows)
Brandied Cherries (recipe follows), drained
3   cups (720 grams) heavy whipping cream
1   teaspoon (3 grams) vanilla extract
½   teaspoon (1.5 grams) kosher salt
¾   cup (150 grams) granulated sugar
5   large egg yolks (93 grams), room temperature
2   large eggs (100 grams), room temperature
Sweetened Whipped Cream (recipe follows)
Garnish: whole fresh cherries

1. On a lightly floured surface, roll Pâte Sablé Crust into a 13-inch circle (about ¼ inch thick) Place onto a piece of parchment paper. Slide onto a baking sheet, and refrigerate until slightly firm, about 15 minutes.
2. Spray a tall-sided 10-inch fluted round removable-bottom tart pan with cooking spray. Transfer Pâte Sablé Crust to tart pan, lightly pressing into bottom and up sides. Trim any excess dough, discarding scraps. (Alternatively, immediately press Pâte Sablé Crust into prepared pan if you do not want to roll it; dough in pan should be ¼ inch thick.) Freeze until hard, about 10 minutes.
3. Preheat oven to 325°F (170°C).
4. Using a fork, dock bottom of prepared crust. Line with a piece of parchment paper, letting ends extend over edges of pan. Add pie weights. Place on rimmed baking sheet.
5. Bake until edges look dry, about 15 minutes. Carefully remove parchment and weights. Bake until crust is dry, 10 to 12 minutes more. Let cool completely on baking sheet. Leave oven on.
6. Place single layer of Brandied Cherries in bottom of cooled prepared crust.
7. In a medium saucepan, heat cream, vanilla, and salt over medium heat just until bubbles form around edges of pan. (Do not boil.) Remove from heat, and let stand for 15 minutes.
8. In a medium bowl, whisk together granulated sugar, egg yolks, and eggs. Add to warm cream mixture, whisking until smooth. Strain through a fine-mesh sieve into a liquid-measuring cup, discarding solids.

9. Place tart pan on baking sheet on oven rack; gently pour filling into prepared crust.
10. Bake until filling is set around edges but still jiggles slightly in center and an instant-read thermometer inserted in center registers 175°F (79°C) to 182°F (82°C), 50 to 55 minutes. Remove from baking sheet, and let cool completely in tart pan on a wire rack. Cover and refrigerate overnight.
11. Gently pat top of tart with a paper towel to remove any moisture, if necessary. Remove from pan, and top with Sweetened Whipped Cream, swirling as desired. Garnish with fresh cherries, if desired.

PÂTE SABLÉE CRUST

Makes 2½ cups

1   cup (227 grams) unsalted butter, softened
⅔   cup (80 grams) confectioners' sugar
1   teaspoon (3 grams) kosher salt
2   large egg yolks (37 grams)
¾   teaspoon (2 grams) vanilla extract
3   cups (375 grams) pastry flour

1. In the bowl of a stand mixer fitted with the paddle attachment, beat butter at medium-low speed until smooth, about 1 minute. Add confectioners' sugar and salt, and beat until smooth, about 1 minute. Add egg yolks, and vanilla, and beat until combined, about 1 minute. Add flour in two additions, beating just until combined. Turn out dough onto a clean surface, and gently knead 3 to 4 times. Shape into disk, and wrap in plastic wrap. Refrigerate for 1 hour.

BRANDIED CHERRIES

Makes 3 cups

⅔   cup (133 grams) granulated sugar
⅔   cup (160 grams) cherry brandy*
2   tablespoons (6 grams) orange zest
3   cups (420 grams) fresh cherries, pitted and quartered

1. In a small saucepan, heat sugar, brandy, and orange zest over low heat, stirring constantly, until sugar dissolves. Add cherries, and cook until softened, 3 to 5 minutes. Gently mash cherries with a fork or a potato masher. Pour into a medium bowl, cover, and refrigerate for up to 4 hours.

We used Luxardo.

SWEETENED WHIPPED CREAM

Makes 2 cups

1   cup (240 grams) cold heavy whipping cream
1   tablespoon (12 grams) granulated sugar

1. In the bowl of a stand mixer fitted with a whisk attachment, beat cold cream at medium-high speed until medium-soft peaks form, about 3 to 5 minutes.

RED VELVET CHEESECAKE TART

Makes 1 (9½-inch) tart

The flavors of red velvet cake meet cheesecake in a showstopping tart. To add an edible optical illusion, the filling is swirled on top, but once sliced it maintains perfect red and white stripes. With a no-bake filling, this tart not only is stunning to look at, but it comes together in record time.

Black Cocoa Tart Dough (recipe follows)

1	cup plus 2 tablespoons (270 grams) cold heavy whipping cream
12	ounces (340 grams) cream cheese, softened
3	tablespoons (45 grams) sour cream, room temperature
¾	cup (150 grams) granulated sugar
¾	teaspoon (3 grams) vanilla extract
½	teaspoon (1.5 grams) kosher salt
½	teaspoon (1 gram) black cocoa powder

Red gel food coloring*

1. Preheat oven to 400°F (200°C).

2. On a lightly floured surface, roll Black Cocoa Pie Dough into a 12-inch circle. Gently transfer to a 9½-inch fluted round removable-bottom tart pan, pressing into bottom and up sides. Trim dough even with edge of pan. Freeze until firm, about 30 minutes.

3. Top Black Cocoa Pie Dough with a piece of parchment paper, letting ends extend over edges of pan. Add pie weights.

4. Bake until edges look dry, 15 to 20 minutes. Carefully remove parchment and weights. Bake until crust is completely dry, 5 to 7 minutes more. Let cool completely on wire rack.

5. In the bowl of a stand mixer fitted with the whisk attachment, beat cream at medium-high until soft peaks form. Transfer to medium bowl.

6. Clean bowl of stand mixer. Using the paddle attachment, beat cream cheese and sour cream at medium speed until smooth, about 3 minutes. Add sugar, vanilla, and salt, and beat at low until combined, stopping to scrape sides of bowl. Fold whipped cream into cream cheese mixture just until combined. Transfer ½ cup (250 grams) batter to a medium bowl; add black cocoa and food coloring, folding just until combined.

7. Place red and white batters in separate large pastry bags; cut a ½-inch opening in tip of each bag. Starting in center of prepared crust, pipe a 2-inch circle of white batter. Pipe a ring of red batter around center circle. Pipe a ring of white batter around red batter. Repeat pattern, alternating batters, until bottom of crust is covered. On top of rings, pipe 1-inch circles, alternating colors, until fully covering rings. Using a wooden pick, swirl batters together as desired. (Be careful not to stick your pick too far into the batter or you will disrupt the rings below). Freeze until center is firm, about 2 hours. Serve cold.

We used Wilton Red Color Right Food Coloring.

BLACK COCOA TART DOUGH
Makes 1 (9½-inch) crust

1½	cups (188 grams) all-purpose flour
¼	cup (50 grams) granulated sugar
¼	cup (21 grams) black cocoa powder
1	teaspoon (3 grams) kosher salt
⅔	cup (150 grams) cold unsalted butter, cut into small cubes
1	large egg (50 grams)

1. In the work bowl of a food processor, place flour, sugar, black cocoa, and salt; pulse until combined. Add cold butter and egg, pulsing until combined and mixture holds together when pressed, about 24 to 30 pulses. Turn out dough onto a lightly floured surface, and shape into a disk. Wrap in plastic wrap, and refrigerate for at least 1 hour.

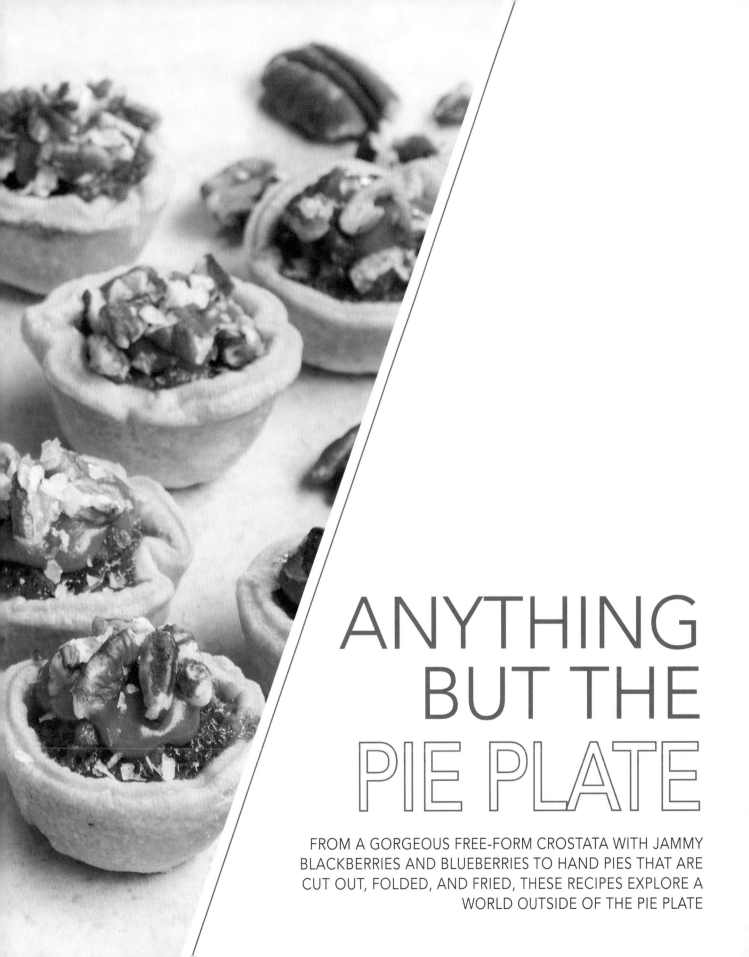

ANYTHING BUT THE
PIE PLATE

FROM A GORGEOUS FREE-FORM CROSTATA WITH JAMMY
BLACKBERRIES AND BLUEBERRIES TO HAND PIES THAT ARE
CUT OUT, FOLDED, AND FRIED, THESE RECIPES EXPLORE A
WORLD OUTSIDE OF THE PIE PLATE

BLACK AND BLUE CROSTATA

Makes 1 (9-inch) crostata

This crostata looks so refined but is remarkably simple to execute. Make the pastry dough a day or two ahead of time to make the process even easier.

¼   cup (50 grams) granulated sugar
Crostata Dough (recipe follows)
¾   cup Quick Blackberry-Blueberry Jam (recipe follows)
¾   cup (128 grams) fresh blackberries
¾   cup (128 grams) fresh blueberries
1   large egg (50 grams), lightly beaten
2   tablespoons (24 grams) turbinado sugar

1. Preheat oven to 375°F (190°C). Line a baking sheet with parchment paper.
2. Sprinkle granulated sugar onto prepared pan. Place Crostata Dough on prepared pan, and roll into a 12-inch circle. Spoon Quick Blackberry-Blueberry Jam into center of dough, leaving a 2-inch border. Top with blackberries and blueberries. Fold dough around berries. Brush edges of dough with egg, and sprinkle with turbinado sugar.
3. Bake until golden brown and bubbly, 35 to 40 minutes; serve warm.

CROSTATA DOUGH
Makes dough for 1 crostata

1⅓   cups (167 grams) all-purpose flour
1   tablespoon (12 grams) granulated sugar
1   teaspoon (3 grams) kosher salt
½   cup (113 grams) cold unsalted butter, cubed
5 to 8 tablespoons (75 to 120 grams) ice water

1. In the work bowl of a food processor, place flour, sugar, and salt; pulse until combined. Add cold butter, and pulse until mixture is crumbly. Add 5 to 8 tablespoons (75 to 120 grams) ice water, 1 tablespoon (15 grams) at a time, just until dough comes together. Shape dough into a disk, and wrap tightly in plastic wrap. Refrigerate for at least 2 hours before using.

QUICK BLACKBERRY-BLUEBERRY JAM
Makes 2 cups

½   pound (226 grams) fresh blackberries
½   pound (226 grams) fresh blueberries
2   cups (400 grams) granulated sugar
2   tablespoons (30 grams) fresh lemon juice

1. In a large saucepan, combine all ingredients. Stir with a wooden spoon, and let stand for 2 hours.
2. Bring berry mixture to a boil over medium-high heat. Cook, stirring frequently, for 5 minutes. Reduce heat to medium; cook, stirring frequently and mashing berries with a potato masher, until mixture thickens, 20 to 45 minutes. Remove from heat, and let cool for 1 hour before transferring to a clean jar. Jam will keep refrigerated for up to 2 weeks.

Note: *The ripeness of berries can affect the cook time of jam. This jam could take anywhere from 20 minutes for very ripe berries to 45 minutes for less-ripe berries. To test your jam for doneness, scrape the bottom of the saucepan with your spoon; if the jam parts for a few seconds, it is ready.*

SATSUMA MARMALADE HAND PIES

Makes about 8 hand pies

Recipe by Rebecca Firth

This combination of slightly bitter marmalade, aromatic five-spice, and buttery crust is spine-tingling. Most marmalade is comprised of the entire fruit. Here, I use only one satsuma in its entirety and utilize the zest and meat of the remaining fruit for a less bitter filling.

⅓ cup (80 grams) cold water
¼ cup (60 grams) cold vodka
3 cups (375 grams) all-purpose flour
2 tablespoons (24 grams) granulated sugar
1 teaspoon (3 grams) kosher salt
1 cup (227 grams) cold unsalted butter, cubed
¼ cup (57 grams) cold all-vegetable shortening
Satsuma Marmalade (recipe follows)
1 large egg yolk (19 grams)
2 tablespoons (30 grams) heavy whipping cream or whole milk

1. In a measuring cup, stir together ⅓ cup (80 grams) cold water and vodka. Freeze for 5 minutes.
2. In a large bowl, whisk together flour, sugar, and salt until combined. Using a pastry blender, cut in cold butter and shortening until mixture is crumbly. (Do not overmix.) Drizzle vodka mixture over flour mixture, and press with the back of a spatula to bring dough together. Using your hands, gently press dough together.
3. Turn out dough, and divide in half. Shape each half into a disk, and wrap tightly in plastic wrap. Refrigerate for at least 1 hour.
4. Preheat oven to 400°F (200°C). Line a baking sheet with parchment paper.
5. Let dough stand at room temperature until slightly softened, about 15 minutes. On a lightly floured surface, roll dough to ¼-inch thickness. Using a 3¾-inch round cutter, cut 16 rounds. Using a small star-shaped cutter, cut centers from half of rounds.
6. Spoon about 1¼ tablespoons (30 grams) Satsuma Marmalade onto center of each solid round, leaving a ½-inch border. Lightly moisten border of each pie, and top with rounds with cutouts. Using the tines of a fork, press down edges to crimp. Place pies on prepared pan, and freeze for 15 minutes.
7. In a small bowl, whisk together egg yolk and cream. Lightly brush egg wash over pies.
8. Bake for 20 to 25 minutes. Let cool before serving.

SATSUMA MARMALADE

Makes about 1½ cups

¾ pound (340 grams) satsumas or tangerines
1 lemon (99 grams)
1½ cups (360 grams) water
1½ cups (300 grams) granulated sugar
2 tablespoons (30 grams) minced peeled apple
1 (1-inch) piece ginger (8 grams), peeled
½ teaspoon (1 gram) Chinese five-spice powder

1. Clean and scrub fruit. Thinly slice 1 whole satsuma (peel plus fruit). Cut slices into quarters, and place in a medium saucepan. Zest remaining satsumas and lemon directly into pan. Remove and discard remaining white satsuma skin, and place fruit in pan. For lemon, remove outer skin, and place residual fruit in pan. Discard any excess pith and seeds.
2. Add 1½ cups (360 grams) water, sugar, apple, ginger, and five-spice powder, and bring to a boil over medium-high heat. Boil until mixture has darkened and thickened, about 35 minutes. Using kitchen shears, cut up any large chunks of fruit into bite-size pieces. Discard ginger. Let cool completely. Refrigerate until chilled.

Photo by Joe Schmelzer

BUTTERMILK SHEET PAN PIE

Makes 1 1 (12x8 ½-inch) pie

For our tangy update on chess pie, we cut the custardy sweetness with a burst of lemon flavor and a dash of nutmeg. For the finishing touch, dust a soft, snowy layer of confectioners' sugar over the top for a simple, rustic look.

4   cups (500 grams) all-purpose flour
¾   cup (170 grams) cold unsalted butter, cubed
½   cup (100 grams) granulated sugar
2   teaspoons (6 grams) kosher salt
1   cup (240 grams) cold water
Buttermilk Filling (recipe follows)
Garnish: confectioners' sugar

1. In the work bowl of a food processor, place flour, cold butter, granulated sugar, and salt; pulse until mixture is crumbly. With processor running, add 1 cup (240 grams) cold water in a slow, steady stream until a dough forms. Divide dough in half, and shape each half into a disk. Wrap in plastic wrap, and refrigerate for at least 30 minutes.
2. Preheat oven to 350°F (180°C).
3. On a lightly floured surface, roll half of dough into a 16x12-inch rectangle. Press dough into bottom and up sides of a 12x8½-inch rimmed baking sheet. Trim excess dough to ½ inch beyond edge of pan. Fold edges under. Prick bottom of dough with a fork.
4. On a lightly floured surface, roll remaining dough to ¼-inch thickness. Using a sharp knife, cut 2 (9x2-inch) strips and 2 (13x1-inch) strips. Brush water on edge of prepared dough in pan. Place dough strips along brushed rim, pressing gently to adhere.
5. Using kitchen scissors, make ½-inch 45-degree cuts around perimeter of dough, being careful not to cut all the way through dough. Alternate folding segments left and right.
6. Pour Buttermilk Filling into prepared crust. Bake for 20 minutes. Cover loosely with foil, and bake until set and light golden brown, 20 to 30 minutes more. Let cool completely on a wire rack. Garnish with confectioners' sugar, if desired. Cover and refrigerate for up to 5 days.

BUTTERMILK FILLING

Makes about 2½ cups

1   cup (200 grams) granulated sugar
3   tablespoons (24 grams) all-purpose flour
1½   tablespoons (13.5 grams) yellow cornmeal
1   teaspoon (3 grams) kosher salt
¼   teaspoon ground nutmeg
5   large eggs (250 grams), room temperature
¾   cup (180 grams) whole buttermilk, room temperature
3   tablespoons (45 grams) plain Greek yogurt
1   tablespoon (6 grams) lemon zest
2   tablespoons (30 grams) fresh lemon juice
⅓   cup (76 grams) unsalted butter, melted and cooled
2   teaspoons (8 grams) vanilla extract

1. In a medium bowl, whisk together sugar, flour, cornmeal, salt, and nutmeg. In another medium bowl, whisk eggs until smooth. Add sugar mixture to eggs, whisking until combined.
2. In a small bowl, whisk together buttermilk, yogurt, and lemon zest and juice until smooth. Add melted butter and vanilla. Gradually add buttermilk mixture to egg mixture, whisking until smooth. Use immediately.

APRICOT-ALMOND HAND PIES

Makes about 14 hand pies

Sliced almonds and cinnamon bring a subtle nuttiness and heat to balance out the concentrated sweetness of the dried apricot filling in these fruity hand pies.

2½   cups (313 grams) all-purpose flour
1   tablespoon (2 grams) fresh thyme leaves
2   teaspoons (6 grams) kosher salt
1   teaspoon (4 grams) granulated sugar
1   cup (227 grams) cold unsalted butter, cubed
1   teaspoon (4 grams) almond extract
4 to 8 tablespoons (60 to 120 grams) ice water
Apricot-Almond Filling (recipe follows)
1   large egg (50 grams)
1   tablespoon (15 grams) water
¼   cup (28 grams) sliced almonds

1. In the work bowl of a food processor, place flour, thyme, salt, and sugar; process until combined. Add cold butter, and pulse until mixture is crumbly. Add almond extract, pulsing until combined. With processor running, add ice water, 1 tablespoon (15 grams) at a time, pulsing just until dough comes together. Turn out dough onto a lightly floured surface. Divide dough in half, and shape each half into a disk. Wrap in plastic wrap, and refrigerate for at least 2 hours.
2. Preheat oven to 350°F (180°C). Line a baking sheet with parchment paper.
3. On a lightly floured surface, roll dough to ¼-inch thickness; cut dough into 4-inch squares. Place 1 tablespoon Apricot-Almond Filling in center of each square. Brush edges of dough with water. Fold dough over filling, creating triangles, and crimp edges with a fork. Cut vents in top of dough to release steam.
4. In a small bowl, whisk together egg and 1 tablespoon (15 grams) water. Brush tops with egg wash, and sprinkle with almonds.
5. Bake until golden brown, about 30 minutes; serve warm.

APRICOT-ALMOND FILLING

Makes about 1¼ cups

6   ounces (175 grams) dried apricots
⅓   cup (67 grams) granulated sugar
1   tablespoon (14 grams) unsalted butter, cubed
¼   teaspoon ground cinnamon
½   cup (57 grams) sliced almonds

1. In a small saucepan, bring apricots and water to cover by 1 inch to a boil over high heat. Reduce heat to low; cook until apricots are softened, about 20 minutes. Drain apricots, reserving 2 tablespoons (30 grams) cooking liquid.
2. In the work bowl of a food processor, place warm apricots, reserved 2 tablespoons (30 grams) cooking liquid, sugar, butter, and cinnamon; pulse until mixture has the texture of jam. Stir in almonds; let cool completely.

BOURBON PECAN GALETTE

Makes 1 (10-inch) galette

Just like the deep-dish pecan pie you love but twice as easy. This filling comes from the brilliant mind of Stephanie Welbourne Steele, digital editor and photographer for Bake from Scratch. She knows that bourbon and a touch of spice go a long way in this pecan galette while light and dark brown sugars add molasses richness.

2   cups (284 grams) pecan halves, toasted and divided
½   cup (113 grams) unsalted butter
½   cup (110 grams) firmly packed light brown sugar
½   cup (110 grams) firmly packed dark brown sugar
½   cup (170 grams) light corn syrup
½   cup (170 grams) dark corn syrup
1½ teaspoons (7.5 grams) bourbon
1½ teaspoons (6 grams) vanilla extract
1   teaspoon (3 grams) kosher salt
½   teaspoon (2 grams) ground cinnamon
All-Butter Galette Dough (recipe follows)
4   large eggs (200 grams), room temperature and divided
2   tablespoons (24 grams) turbinado sugar

1. Preheat oven to 375°F (190°C). Spray a 10-inch cast-iron skillet with baking spray with flour.

2. Roughly chop 1½ cups (213 grams) pecan halves.

3. In a medium saucepan, melt butter over medium heat; bring to a boil. Whisk in brown sugars and corn syrups. Cook until sugars dissolves and syrups are combined, 1 to 2 minutes. Whisk in bourbon, vanilla, salt, and cinnamon, and cook for 1 minute. Remove from heat, and stir in chopped pecans. Let cool for at least 5 minutes.

4. On a lightly floured surface, roll All-Butter Pie Dough into a 12-inch circle. Transfer to prepared skillet, letting excess dough go up and over sides.

5. In medium bowl, lightly whisk 3 eggs (150 grams). Slowly whisk into slightly cooled pecan filling. Pour into prepared crust, and fold edges of dough over filling, lightly pinching folds so filling does not leak. Place remaining ½ cup (71 grams) pecans halves in a concentric circle on top of filling.

6. In a small bowl, lightly whisk remaining 1 egg (50 grams). Brush dough with egg wash, and sprinkle with turbinado sugar.

7. Bake until lightly golden brown and an instant-read thermometer inserted in center registers 200°F (93°C), 55 minutes to 1 hour, covering with foil after 40 minutes of baking to prevent excess browning. Let cool on a wire rack for at least 20 minutes. Serve warm or at room temperature.

All-Butter Galette Dough
Makes 1 (10-inch) crust

2½ cups (313 grams) all-purpose flour
1½ teaspoons (6 grams) granulated sugar
1   teaspoon (3 grams) kosher salt
1   cup (227 grams) cold unsalted butter, cubed
5 to 6 tablespoons (75 to 90 grams) ice water

1. In the work bowl of a food processor, place flour, sugar, and salt; pulse until combined. Add cold butter, and pulse until mixture is crumbly and butter is pea-size. With processor running, add 5 tablespoons (75 grams) ice water in a slow, steady stream until dough starts to come together but is not sticky; add up to remaining 1 tablespoon (15 grams) ice water, 1 teaspoon (5 grams) at a time, if needed. Turn out dough, and shape into a disk. Wrap in plastic wrap, and refrigerate for at least 30 minutes.

ORANGE AND PISTACHIO STRAWBERRY TART

Makes 1 (9-inch) tart

Sweet strawberries and a hint of cardamom balance the classic bright and nutty combination of orange and pistachio in this tart.

1⅓ cups (167 grams) all-purpose flour
¾ cup (85 grams) roasted pistachios
½ cup (60 grams) confectioners' sugar
½ teaspoon (1.5 grams) kosher salt
½ cup (113 grams) cold unsalted butter, cubed
1 large egg (50 grams)
1 teaspoon (4 grams) orange blossom water
½ teaspoon (1 gram) orange zest
Orange Pastry Cream (recipe follows)
4 cups (680 grams) fresh strawberries, hulled and halved

1. In the work bowl of a food processor, pulse together flour, pistachios, confectioners' sugar, and salt until pistachios are ground into a meal. Add cold butter, and pulse until pea-size crumbs remain.
2. In a small bowl, whisk together egg, orange blossom water, and zest. With processor running, add egg mixture in a slow, steady stream just until dough comes together. Turn out dough, and shape into a disk. Wrap in plastic wrap, and refrigerate for at least 1 hour.
3. Butter and flour a 9-inch fluted round removable-bottom tart pan.
4. On a lightly floured surface, roll dough into a 12-inch circle. Transfer to prepared pan, pressing into bottom and up sides. Trim excess dough. Prick bottom and sides of dough with a fork. Freeze for 15 minutes.
5. Preheat oven to 350°F (180°C).
6. Top dough with a piece of parchment paper, letting ends extend over edges of pan. Add pie weights.
7. Bake until edges are set, about 15 minutes. Carefully remove paper and weights. Bake until crust is golden brown, about 10 minutes more. Let cool completely on a wire rack. Spoon Orange Pastry Cream into prepared crust, and spread to edges. Top with strawberries before serving.

ORANGE PASTRY CREAM
Makes about 2 cups

1½ cups (360 grams) heavy whipping cream
¾ cup (180 grams) whole milk
2 tablespoons (12 grams) orange zest
1 teaspoon (3 grams) cardamom seeds
1 large egg (50 grams)
2 large egg yolks (37 grams)
¼ cup plus 2 tablespoons (83 grams) firmly packed light brown sugar
4½ tablespoons (36 grams) cornstarch
2 tablespoons (28 grams) unsalted butter, softened

1. In a medium saucepan, bring cream, milk, zest, and cardamom seeds to a boil over medium heat. Remove from heat; cover and steep for 20 minutes. Strain cream mixture, gently pressing on solids. Return mixture to pan, and return to a boil over medium heat.
2. In a medium bowl, whisk together egg, egg yolks, brown sugar, and cornstarch. Gradually add hot milk mixture to egg mixture, whisking constantly. Return milk mixture to saucepan, and cook, whisking constantly, until thickened. Pour through a fine-mesh sieve into a bowl, discarding solids. Stir in butter until melted. Cover surface of cream directly with plastic wrap, and refrigerate for 1 hour.

DOUBLE-BERRY HAND PIES

Makes about 8 hand pies

Juicy hand pies bursting with a double berry filling are held together with a buttery strawberry-scented pie dough.

Strawberry Pie Dough (recipe follows)
1   cup (152 grams) quartered fresh strawberries
¾   cup (128 grams) fresh blueberries
2   tablespoons (28 grams) firmly packed light brown sugar
2   tablespoons (16 grams) all-purpose flour
1   teaspoon (1 gram) lemon zest
1   tablespoon (15 grams) fresh lemon juice
1   teaspoon chopped fresh thyme
¼   teaspoon kosher salt
1   large egg (50 grams)
1   tablespoon (15 grams) water
2   tablespoons (24 grams) turbinado sugar
Strawberry Balsamic Reduction (recipe follows)

1. Line 2 baking sheets with parchment paper.
2. Roll half of Strawberry Pie Dough to ⅛-inch thickness. Using a 4½-inch round cutter, cut dough, rerolling scraps only once. Repeat with remaining Strawberry Pie Dough. Place rounds between sheets of parchment paper, and refrigerate for 5 to 7 minutes.
3. In a medium bowl, stir together strawberries, blueberries, brown sugar, flour, lemon zest and juice, thyme, and salt. In a small bowl, whisk together egg and 1 tablespoon (15 grams) water. Brush edges of dough with egg wash. Place 1½ tablespoons berry mixture in center of half of rounds. Top with remaining rounds, and press edges with a fork to seal. Place on prepared pans, and freeze for 15 minutes.
4. Preheat oven to 375°F (190°C).
5. Brush frozen hand pies with egg wash, and sprinkle with turbinado sugar. Cut small vents in top of dough to release steam.
6. Bake until golden brown, about 20 minutes. Drizzle with Strawberry Balsamic Reduction. Serve warm.

STRAWBERRY PIE DOUGH

Makes dough for 8 hand pies

2½   cups (313 grams) all-purpose flour
½   cup (8 grams) freeze-dried strawberries
1   tablespoon (2 grams) fresh thyme leaves
1   teaspoon (3 grams) kosher salt
1   teaspoon (4 grams) granulated sugar
1   cup (227 grams) cold unsalted butter, cubed
4 to 8 tablespoons (60 to 120 grams) ice water

1. In the work bowl of a food processor, place flour, freeze-dried strawberries, thyme, salt, and sugar; process until well combined. Add cold butter, and pulse until mixture is crumbly. With processor running, add ice water, 1 tablespoon (15 grams) at a time, just until dough comes together.
2. Turn out dough onto a lightly floured surface, and divide in half. Shape each half into a disk, and wrap in plastic wrap. Refrigerate for at least 2 hours.

STRAWBERRY BALSAMIC REDUCTION

Makes about 1 cup

⅓   cup (80 grams) white balsamic vinegar
1⅓   cups (202 grams) quartered fresh strawberries
2   tablespoons (28 grams) firmly packed light brown sugar
¼   teaspoon kosher salt
¼   teaspoon lemon zest

1. In a small saucepan, bring vinegar to a boil over medium heat. Reduce heat to low; simmer until slightly thickened, 2 to 4 minutes. Stir in strawberries, brown sugar, salt, and zest. Increase heat to medium, and bring to a boil. Reduce heat to low; simmer until strawberries have released their juices and softened, about 5 minutes.
2. Using the back of a wooden spoon, crush strawberries against sides of pan. Continue simmering until sauce has thickened slightly. Remove from heat, and transfer to the container of a blender; purée until smooth. Let cool completely. Refrigerate in an airtight container for up to 6 days.

FRIED APPLE HAND PIES

Makes about 20 hand pies

It is a truth universally acknowledged in the Deep South: Everything is better fried. Apple pie is no exception. These half-moon pastries take all that is good about the original and add a hefty dose of crispy, crunchy (and cinnamon sugar-coated) crust by deep-frying them.

1⅓   cups (267 grams) granulated sugar, divided
⅓   cup (73 grams) firmly packed light brown sugar
3   tablespoons (24 grams) cornstarch
1   teaspoon (3 grams) apple pie spice
¼   teaspoon kosher salt
4   cups (525 grams) diced peeled Gala or Fuji apples
      (about 2½ pounds)
1   tablespoon (15 grams) fresh lemon juice
Piecrust Dough (recipe follows)
1   large egg (50 grams)
1   tablespoon (15 grams) water
1   gallon (3,790 grams) peanut oil
1   tablespoon (6 grams) ground cinnamon

1. In a large skillet, whisk together ⅓ cup (67 grams) granulated sugar, brown sugar, cornstarch, apple pie spice, and salt. Add apples and lemon juice, tossing to coat. Cook over medium heat until apples are tender and filling is thickened, about 20 minutes. Let cool for 10 minutes.
2. Let Piecrust Dough stand at room temperature until slightly softened, about 15 minutes. On a lightly floured surface, roll half of dough to ⅛-inch thickness. Using a 4½-inch round cutter, cut dough, rerolling scraps only once. Repeat with remaining dough.

3. In a small bowl, whisk together egg and 1 tablespoon (15 grams) water. Brush edges of dough with egg wash. Place 2 teaspoons filling in center of each round. Fold dough over filling. Crimp from center to edges, gently pressing in any filling as you go. Pick up and pinch edges to seal. Freeze for 20 minutes.
4. In a large stockpot, heat oil over medium-high heat until a deep-fry thermometer registers 360°F (182°C). Place paper towels on a wire rack.
5. In a small bowl, whisk together cinnamon and remaining 1 cup (200 grams) granulated sugar.
6. Working in batches, fry hand pies until golden brown, 5 to 7 minutes. Carefully remove from hot oil, and immediately toss in cinnamon sugar mixture. Let drain on prepared rack. Serve warm.

PIECRUST DOUGH
Makes 1 (9-inch) double crust

4   cups (500 grams) all-purpose flour
½   cup (100 grams) granulated sugar
½   teaspoon (1.5 grams) kosher salt
¾   cup (170 grams) cold unsalted butter, cubed
¾   cup (180 grams) ice water

1. In the work bowl of a food processor, place flour, sugar, and salt; pulse until combined. Add cold butter, and pulse until mixture is crumbly. With processor running, add ¾ cup (180 grams) ice water in a slow, steady stream until a dough forms.
2. Turn out dough onto a lightly floured surface, and divide in half. Shape each half into a disk, and wrap tightly in plastic wrap. Refrigerate for at least 30 minutes or overnight.

FRUIT TARTLETS

Makes 12 tartlets

Inverting the muffin pan to bake this Tart Dough on the outside of the muffin cups gives the shells defined shape and flaky texture. Top your tartlets with whichever berries or sliced fruit you like. The Tart Dough is made with the stand mixer, ensuring that the dough comes together gently, and without excess handling.

Tart Dough (recipe follows)
Pastry Cream (recipe follows)
4   cups (about 560 grams) assorted fresh berries (such as blackberries, blueberries, and raspberries)
½   cup (160 grams) apricot preserves
1   tablespoon (15 grams) water

1. Preheat oven to 350°F (180°C). Invert a 12-cup muffin pan.
2. On a lightly floured surface, roll Tart Dough to ⅛-inch thickness. Using a 3¾- to 4-inch fluted round cutter*, cut 12 rounds (about 16 grams each), rerolling scraps as necessary. Drape 1 round onto bottom of each muffin cup. Prick each several times with a fork.
3. Bake until crusts are golden brown, 15 to 18 minutes. Let cool on pan for 10 minutes. Remove from pan, and let cool completely on a wire rack.
4. Pipe about ¼ cup (85 grams) Pastry Cream into each prepared tart shell. Top with desired berries.
5. In a small microwave-safe bowl, heat preserves and 1 tablespoon (15 grams) water just until bubbly; stir until combined. Strain mixture through a medium-mesh sieve. Carefully brush mixture onto fruit. Serve immediately.

Fluted pastry cutters will work fine, but we chose to cut our pastry with an inverted 3⅞-inch fluted tart pan for a prettier scallop design.

TART DOUGH
Makes dough for 12 tartlets

½   cup (113 grams) cold unsalted butter
1⅓   cups all-purpose flour (167 grams)
1   tablespoon (12 grams) granulated sugar
1   teaspoon (3 grams) kosher salt
1½   tablespoons (22.5 grams) whole milk
1   large egg yolk (19 grams)

1. Cut butter into ¼-inch cubes. Freeze until firm, about 10 minutes.
2. In the bowl of a stand mixer fitted with the paddle attachment, stir together flour, sugar, and salt by hand. Add frozen butter, and beat at low speed until butter is broken into small pieces, 1 to 2 minutes. (If any large pieces of butter remain, squeeze between fingers to break up.)
3. In a 1-cup liquid-measuring cup, whisk together milk and egg yolk. With mixer on lowest speed, add milk mixture to flour mixture, beating just until moist clumps form. Transfer mixture to a large piece of plastic wrap. Using your hands, bring mixture together to form a cohesive dough. (It is fine if there are visible pieces of butter—they help create a flakier crust.) Shape dough into a disk, and wrap in plastic wrap. Refrigerate for at least 1 hour or overnight. (Dough can be made ahead and refrigerated for up to 3 days or frozen for up to 1 month.)

PASTRY CREAM
Makes about 3 cups

3   cups (720 grams) whole milk
1   cup (200 grams) granulated sugar, divided
1   teaspoon (6 grams) vanilla bean paste
8   large egg yolks (149 grams)
¼   cup plus 3 tablespoons (56 grams) cornstarch
¼   teaspoon kosher salt
¼   cup (57 grams) unsalted butter, softened

1. In a large saucepan, whisk together milk, ½ cup (100 grams) sugar, and vanilla bean paste. Heat over medium heat until steaming.
2. In a large bowl, whisk together egg yolks, cornstarch, salt, and remaining ½ cup (100 grams) sugar. Gradually add warm milk mixture to egg yolk mixture, whisking constantly. Pour mixture back into saucepan, and cook over medium heat, whisking constantly, until thickened and bubbly, 4 to 5 minutes. Cook until cornstarch flavor has cooked out, about 1 minute.
3. Strain mixture through a fine-mesh sieve into a large bowl. Stir in butter in two additions. Cover with a piece of plastic wrap, pressing wrap directly onto surface of cream to prevent a skin from forming. Refrigerate until cold. Whisk until smooth before using.

PECAN CARAMEL TASSIES

Makes 24 tassies

Offering sweet and simple satisfaction, there's no denying that pecan tassies are a holiday must-bake. Pecans are the secret ingredient behind these rich bites, adding irresistible crunch to the pecan pie filling and nutty notes that harmonize with the luscious caramel topping. Sprinkled with a pinch of sea salt, these classic treats will go so fast at your next holiday party that you may want to bake a double batch.

½ cup (113 grams) unsalted butter, softened
3 ounces (86 grams) cream cheese, softened
2 teaspoons (8 grams) vanilla extract, divided
1½ cups (188 grams) all-purpose flour
¾ teaspoon (1.5 grams) kosher salt, divided
¼ cup (55 grams) firmly packed dark brown sugar
¼ cup (42 grams) light corn syrup
1 tablespoon (14 grams) unsalted butter, melted
1 large egg (50 grams)
¾ cup (90 grams) pecan pieces*
Caramel Sauce (recipe follows)
Garnish: pecan pieces, flaked sea salt

1. In the bowl of a stand mixer fitted with the paddle attachment, beat softened butter and cream cheese at medium speed until smooth. Beat in ½ teaspoon (2 grams) vanilla. With mixer on low speed, gradually add flour and ½ teaspoon (1.5 grams) kosher salt, beating until combined. Shape dough into a disk, and wrap in plastic wrap. Refrigerate for at least 30 minutes.
2. Preheat oven to 350°F (180°C). Spray a 24-cup mini muffin pan with cooking spray.
3. On a lightly floured surface, roll dough to about ⅛-inch thickness. Using a 2¾-inch round cutter, cut dough, rerolling scraps as needed. Place a round in each prepared muffin cup, pressing into bottom and up sides. Freeze while preparing filling. (Alternatively, divide dough into 24 portions [about 16 grams each]; roll into a ball, and press into bottom and up sides of each muffin cup, trimming excess dough as needed.)
4. In a medium bowl, whisk together brown sugar, corn syrup, and melted butter until smooth. Add egg and remaining ¼ teaspoon kosher salt, whisking until combined.

5. Sprinkle pecan pieces evenly in each prepared crust. Pour sugar mixture over pecans, filling each cup three-fourths full.
6. Bake until filling is set and an instant-read thermometer inserted in center registers 200°F (93°C), about 25 minutes. Let cool in pan for 10 minutes. Remove from pan, and let cool completely on a wire rack.
7. Place Caramel Sauce in a piping bag. Cut a ¼-inch opening, and pipe sauce on top of pecan filling. Garnish with pecan pieces and sea salt, if desired.

We used Sunnyland Farms Small Pecan Pieces.

Note: *Dough can be made ahead of time. If chilled for a long period of time, let dough stand at room temperature for 15 to 20 minutes before rolling.*

CARAMEL SAUCE
Makes about 1⅓ cups

1 cup (200 grams) granulated sugar
4 tablespoons (60 grams) water, divided
½ cup (120 grams) warm heavy whipping cream
6 tablespoons (84 grams) unsalted butter, cubed and softened

1. In a medium saucepan, heat sugar and 3 tablespoons (45 grams) water over medium heat until sugar is dissolved. Increase heat to high, and use remaining 1 tablespoon (15 grams) water to brush down sides of pan. (Do not stir once it starts to boil.) Cook until desired light amber color is reached. Remove from heat; slowly add warm cream, whisking to combine. Add butter, a few pieces at a time, whisking until combined. Let cool completely.

[anything but the pie plate]

PEAR AND HONEYED GOAT CHEESE GALETTE

Makes 1 (10-inch) galette

It's time to up your galette game. This buttery beauty is great for breakfast or cocktail hour. A sugared golden crust encircles warm, tangy goat cheese topped with sweet Bosc pears, which bake into a deep rustic hue. Thanks to the layered pears, the gorgeous design is effortless and accentuates the fruit's natural shape.

2	cups (250 grams) all-purpose flour
1	teaspoon (3 grams) kosher salt
¾	cup (170 grams) cold unsalted butter, cubed
4	ounces (115 grams) cold goat cheese
1	tablespoon (15 grams) apple cider vinegar
2	tablespoons (30 grams) ice water

Honeyed Goat Cheese Filling (recipe follows)

3	slightly firm medium Bosc pears (537 grams)
1	large egg (50 grams)
1	tablespoon (15 grams) water
1	tablespoon (12 grams) granulated sugar

Garnish: clover honey, fresh rosemary

1. In the work bowl of a food processor, place flour and salt; pulse until combined. Add cold butter and cold goat cheese, and pulse until mixture is crumbly. Add vinegar, pulsing until combined. With processor running, add 2 tablespoons (30 grams) ice water, 1 tablespoon (15 grams) at a time, just until dough comes together. Turn out dough, and shape into a disk. Wrap tightly in plastic wrap, and refrigerate for at least 30 minutes.

2. Preheat oven to 425°F (220°C). Line a baking sheet with parchment paper.
3. On a lightly floured surface, roll dough into a 14-inch circle, about ¼ inch thick. Transfer to prepared pan. Spread Honeyed Goat Cheese Filling onto dough, leaving a 2-inch border.
4. Cut pears in half vertically through stems. Scoop out core of each half. Place pears cut side down, and cut into thin slices, leaving about ½ inch intact below stem. Fan pears out, and place on top of filling, overlapping as needed. Fold edges of dough over pears.
5. In a small bowl, whisk together egg and 1 tablespoon (15 grams) water. Brush egg wash onto dough, and sprinkle with sugar.
6. Bake until crust is golden and bottom is browned, 25 to 35 minutes. Let cool on pan for 10 minutes. Garnish with honey and rosemary, if desired. Serve warm or at room temperature.

HONEYED GOAT CHEESE FILLING
Makes ¾ cup

6	ounces (175 grams) goat cheese
3	tablespoons (63 grams) clover honey
1½	tablespoons (21 grams) firmly packed light brown sugar
¼	teaspoon ground nutmeg

1. In a medium bowl, whisk together goat cheese and honey until smooth. Whisk in brown sugar and nutmeg. Use immediately, or refrigerate until ready to use.

JAM AND CREAM BRIOCHE TART

Makes 1 (9-inch) tart

In a 1997 episode of Julia Child's Baking with Julia, *Nancy Silverton baked a brioche tart that was so good it made Julia cry. In our take on this groundbreaking dessert, we filled a pillowy brioche "crust" with velvety cream cheese custard and swirled it with fruit preserves. Finished off with crunchy pearl sugar, this stunner might just make you shed a tear, too.*

2¾ cups (344 grams) all-purpose flour
3 tablespoons (36 grams) granulated sugar
2¼ teaspoons (7 grams) instant yeast
1½ teaspoons (4.5 grams) kosher salt
⅓ cup plus 1 tablespoon (95 grams) warm whole milk (120°F/49°C to 130°F/54°C)
3 large eggs (150 grams), room temperature and divided
1 teaspoon (4 grams) vanilla extract
6 tablespoons (84 grams) unsalted butter, softened
Cream Cheese Filling (recipe follows)
2 tablespoons (40 grams) fruit preserves*
1 tablespoon (15 grams) water
1½ tablespoons (18 grams) Swedish pearl sugar

1. In the bowl of a stand mixer fitted with the paddle attachment, beat flour, granulated sugar, yeast, and salt at very low speed until combined, about 30 seconds. Slowly add warm milk, and beat at medium speed until combined. Add 2 eggs (100 grams) and vanilla, and beat until combined, about 1 minute.
2. Switch to the dough hook attachment. Beat at low speed until smooth and elastic, about 8 minutes. Add butter, 1 tablespoon (14 grams) at a time, beating until combined after each addition, about 8 minutes total. Beat until a smooth and elastic dough forms, about 6 minutes. Turn out dough onto a lightly floured surface, and knead 4 to 5 times. Shape dough into a smooth round.
3. Spray a large bowl with cooking spray. Place dough in bowl, turning to grease top. Cover and let rise in a warm, draft-free place (75°F/24°C) until doubled in size, 30 to 45 minutes.
4. Spray a 9-inch square baking pan with cooking spray. Line pan with parchment paper, letting excess extend over sides of pan.

5. On a lightly floured surface, roll dough into an 11-inch square. Score a 9-inch square in center of dough. Fold outside 2 inches over score mark, creating a crust around edges. Lift dough, and place in prepared pan, making sure dough is even and fills corners of pan. Cover and let rise until puffed, 20 to 30 minutes.
6. Preheat oven to 325°F (170°C).
7. Using your fingertips, dimple center of dough back down, leaving outside crust as is. Pour Cream Cheese Filling into center of dough. Make small indentations in Cream Cheese Filling. Fill indentations with teaspoonfuls of preserves. Using a knife, swirl preserves into Cream Cheese Filling.
8. In a small bowl, whisk together 1 tablespoon (15 grams) water and remaining 1 egg (50 grams). Brush dough with egg wash, and sprinkle with pearl sugar.
9. Bake until crust is golden brown, filling is set around outside edges and slightly jiggly in center, and an instant-read thermometer inserted in center registers 175°F (79°C), 35 to 40 minutes. Let cool in pan for 10 minutes. Using excess parchment as handles, remove from pan. Serve warm, or let cool completely on a wire rack.

We used Bonne Maman Four Fruits Preserves.

CREAM CHEESE FILLING
Makes 1½ cups

2 tablespoons (28 grams) unsalted butter, softened
⅓ cup (67 grams) granulated sugar
1 teaspoon (6 grams) vanilla bean paste
¼ teaspoon kosher salt
8 ounces (225 grams) cream cheese, softened
1 large egg (50 grams), room temperature
3 tablespoons (24 grams) all-purpose flour

1. In the bowl of a stand mixer fitted with the paddle attachment, beat butter, sugar, vanilla bean paste, and salt at medium speed until well combined. Gradually add cream cheese, beating until smooth. Add egg, beating until combined. Beat in flour.

VANILLA MILK RUFFLE PIE

Makes 1 (9-inch) pie

Filled with velvety vanilla custard, this pie triumphs in texture and taste. Shape the phyllo rosettes in the palm of your hand with one quick motion.

8   sheets frozen phyllo pastry*, thawed
¼   cup plus 3 tablespoons (99 grams) unsalted butter, melted
3   large eggs (150 grams), room temperature
½   cup (100 grams) granulated sugar
½   teaspoon (1.5 grams) kosher salt
¼   teaspoon ground cinnamon
1   cup (240 grams) whole milk
½   cup (120 grams) heavy whipping cream
1   tablespoon (18 grams) vanilla bean paste
1   tablespoon (13 grams) vanilla extract
Garnish: confectioners' sugar

1. Preheat oven to 350°F (180°C). Butter a 9-inch round cake pan. Line bottom of pan with parchment paper (see Note); butter parchment.
2. Place thawed pastry sheets on a work surface. Keep covered with wax paper while working. (You can also cover pastry sheets with plastic wrap topped with damp paper towels.) Place 1 pastry sheet on counter, and brush with melted butter. Using your fingers, ruffle dough by pinching along the long side. (It will look like a fan. Do not worry if it tears.) Starting at one end, shape into a tight spiral, and place in center of prepared pan. Repeat with remaining sheets, and place around center spiral.
3. Bake until golden brown, 20 to 25 minutes. Let cool for 10 minutes while preparing custard.

4. In a medium bowl, whisk together eggs, granulated sugar, salt, and cinnamon.
5. In a small saucepan, heat milk, cream, and vanilla bean paste over medium-high heat until steaming. Add a small amount of hot milk mixture to egg mixture, whisking constantly. Slowly add remaining hot milk mixture, whisking to combine. Whisk in vanilla extract. Pour mixture over baked phyllo dough.
6. Bake until center is set and an instant-read thermometer inserted in center registers 170°F (77°C), 15 to 20 minutes. Serve warm or at room temperature. Garnish with confectioners' sugar, if desired.

*We used The Fillo Factory 13x18-inch phyllo pastry sheets, available at Whole Foods, and thawed according to package directions.

Note: *If you want to be able to remove the pie from the pan to serve, take 2 strips of parchment paper, and cross them in the middle of the bottom of prepared pan. Let excess parchment extend up sides of pan to be used as handles; line bottom of pan.*

BLUEBERRY-ALMOND GALETTES

Makes 3 (7-inch) galettes

Almond flour is finer than standard all-purpose. It absorbs more moisture from the dough, giving the buttermilk crusts of these galettes added crispness. A hint of tart lemon zest balances out the sweetness of the blueberries.

2   cups (192 grams) almond flour
1¾   cups (219 grams) all-purpose flour
½   cup (100 grams) plus 2 tablespoons (24 grams) granulated sugar, divided
1½   teaspoons (4.5 grams) kosher salt
1   cup (227 grams) unsalted butter, softened
2   tablespoons (30 grams) whole buttermilk
2   tablespoons (30 grams) cold water
5¼   cups (893 grams) fresh blueberries, divided
3   tablespoons (24 grams) cornstarch
1   teaspoon (2 grams) lemon zest
1   tablespoon (15 grams) fresh lemon juice
1   large egg (50 grams), lightly beaten
2   tablespoons (24 grams) turbinado sugar

1. In the work bowl of a food processor, place flours, 2 tablespoons (24 grams) granulated sugar, and salt; process until combined. Add butter, and pulse until mixture is crumbly.

2. In a small bowl, stir together buttermilk and 2 tablespoons (30 grams) cold water. With processor running, add buttermilk mixture in a slow, steady stream just until dough comes together but is not sticky. Shape dough into a disk, and wrap in plastic wrap. Refrigerate for at least 30 minutes.

3. In a large bowl, combine 1 cup (170 grams) blueberries, cornstarch, lemon zest and juice, and remaining ½ cup (100 grams) granulated sugar. With a fork or potato masher, crush blueberries. Stir in remaining 4¼ cups (723 grams) blueberries.

4. Preheat oven to 400°F (200°C). Line 2 rimmed baking sheets with parchment paper.

5. Divide dough into 3 equal pieces. On a lightly floured surface, roll each piece into a 9-inch circle. Trim edges of dough, and transfer to prepared pans. Spoon one-third of blueberry mixture into center of each circle, leaving a 2-inch border. Fold up dough around filling, pinching to seal edges of folds. (Filling will spill out if not sealed properly. See Note.) Brush edges of dough with egg, and sprinkle with turbinado sugar. Freeze for 10 minutes.

6. Bake for 10 minutes. Reduce oven temperature to 350°F (180°C), and bake until crust is golden brown and fruit is bubbly, 20 to 25 minutes more, loosely covering with foil to prevent excess browning, if necessary. Let cool on pans for 25 minutes before serving.

Note: *This dough is less pliable than a typical galette due to the different structure of almond flour. Folding may be more difficult, which is why it is so important to pinch the seams before baking.*

PRO TIP
Use almond flour made from blanched whole almonds. Flour made with unblanched almonds will give your baked good a slightly grainier texture and darker color.

---

recipe index

Credits

Editorial
Editor-in-Chief: Brian Hart Hoffman
VP/Culinary & Custom Content: Brooke
  Michael Bell
Group Creative Director: Deanna Rippy
  Gardner
Art Director: Kelly Redding
Managing Editor: Kyle Grace Mills
Baking & Pastry Editor: Tricia Manzanero
  Stuedeman
Assistant Editor: Sandi Shriver
Editorial Assistants: Alex Kolar,
  Hannah Pellicer
Copy Editor: Meg Lundberg

Cover
Photography by Stephanie Welbourne
  Steele
Food Styling by Megan Lankford
Styling by Mary Beth Jones

***Bake from Scratch* Photographers**
Jim Bathie, Mac Jamieson,
Stephanie Welbourne Steele

Test Kitchen Director
Laura Crandall

***Bake from Scratch* Food Stylists/Recipe
Developers**
Becca Cummins, Kathleen Kanen,
Megan Lankford, Leah Perez, Vanessa
Rocchio, Tricia Manzanero Stuedeman,
Izzie Turner

***Bake from Scratch* Stylists**
Courtni Bodiford, Sidney Bragiel,
Lucy Finney, Mary Beth Jones,
Lily Simpson, Melissa Sturdivant Smith,
Dorothy Walton

Contributing Photographers
Matt Armendariz, Stephen DeVries,
Allie Roomberg, Joe Schmelzer,
Maya Visnyei, Mark Weinberg

**Contributing Food Stylists/Recipe
Developers**
Marian Cooper Cairns, Rebecca Firth,
Lisa Heathcote, Erin Jeanne McDowell,
Ben Mims, Allie Roomberg, Jesse
Szewczyk, Emily Turner